.net Guide #4

All you need to know about
Teleworking

the internet magazine

.net Guide #4

All you need to know about
Teleworking

by Simon Cooke

Future Publishing Limited
Beauford Court
30 Monmouth Street
Bath
Avon BA1 2BW

http://www.futurenet.co.uk

.net Guide #4 All you need to know about Teleworking
Copyright 1995 Future Publishing Limited. All rights reserved. No part of this publication may be reproduced in any form except as permitted by the Copyright Designs and Patents Act 1988. Enquiries for permission to reproduce material should be directed to the publisher.

 **Future Publishing Limited**, Beauford Court, 30 Monmouth Street, Bath, Avon BA1 2BW

ISBN 1-898275-34-3

British Library Cataloguing in Publication Data
A CIP catalogue record for this book is available from the British Library

Author Simon Cooke

Series Editor Davey Winder

Book Editor Rod Lawton

Book Design Rod Lawton

Subbing and layout Steve Faragher

Cover origination Nick Aspell

Printed and bound by Redwood Books

All trademarks are acknowledged to be the property of their respective owners.

Although every care has been taken by the Author in the preparation of this book, no warranty is given by either the Author or the Publisher as to the accuracy or completeness of the information contained within it and neither the Author nor the Publisher shall be responsible or liable for any loss or damage whatsoever arising by virtue of such information or any instructions or advice contained within this book or by any of the aforementioned.

Contents

About the author viii

How to use this book viii

Chapter 1
Introduction 1
    What is teleworking? 2
    Why should I want to do it? 4
    Who else is doing it? 6

Chapter 2
Getting started 7
    What is a modem? 8
    Modem checklist 14
    Installing a modem 15
    What software do I need? 17
    Using a modem 19
    Making sure it all works 22
    Hayes/AT commands 23
    Dialling and connecting 25
    Sending and receiving files 26

Chapter 3
The Internet 31
    It won't bite me, will it? 32
    A brief history 33
    What use is it to me? 35
    Internet addresses 37

Electronic mail 40
Email addresses 41
Using email...42
Sending and receiving files...44
Sending files via email...45
Transferring files using ftp 46
Searching for files with Archive 49
Information on the Net...50
Mailing lists...50
Usenet 51
World Wide Web 53
Telnet..54
Searching for information 55
Different types of Internet connection..........................57
Software tools for using the Net....................................58
Getting on to the Internet..59

Chapter 4
BBSs and on-line services 63
Bulletin board systems 64
On-line services..66
Cix 68
CompuServe 69
Delphi Internet...71

Chapter 5
Real World Considerations.........................73
Being legal and decent...74
Be assured you're insured..78
The taxman cometh...80
Constructing your home office 82
Choosing a computer 87
A telephone line...89
ISDN..90

 .net Guide

Contents

Chapter 6
Where Do I Go From Here?........................93

Chapter 7
A Teleworkers Directory 97
- Real world resource guide 98
- On-line resource guide 101
- Internet Directory..101
- Usenet newsgroups..106
- BT Phonebase 107
- On-line services Directory..107

Chapter 8
Reference section 109
- Care in the (on-line) community 110
- Smiley dictionary 112
- Acronym dictionary..116
- Glossary 121

Index 155

Other Internet books 161

About the author

Simon Cooke lives on the faraway lands of the Isle of Wight, with Karen and three cats. As well as books, Simon has also written computer games for a living, but is now specialising in digital image generation. Predictably, he enjoys everything to do with computers, programming them, reading about them, eating them – whatever. Needless to say, he reads science-fiction novels and loves watching movies of all kinds. Despite this, he insists he is interesting, but this seems doubtful.

He continually marvels at how one of his cats, Loki, makes being black, shiny and wicked an art form – and is waiting for the day his mothership will land and take him back.

Dedication

For Karen – grumpy boots and all.

A big thanks to Davey 'Willy' Winder for making it happen, and for being more of a friend than you could shake a stick at. Thanks also to Yvonne 'Bonny' Winder for making him so dribblingly happy. Huge hugs and thanks to Karen for correcting my many mistakes, and for putting up with me. Last but certainly not least, thanks go to my parents for all their support and help over the years – and for buying me my first computer (it's all your fault!).

How to use this book

.net Guide #4 All you need to know about Teleworking is one of a series of Internet books designed to focus on the needs of real Internet users.

For a full list of the books in this series – and details of other Internet publications we do – see the back of this book.

All of our Internet books are written in plain English for people who are more interested in the Net than computers. And to make it even easier, we've included icons in the margins to draw your attention to especially important pieces of information. Here are the icons, together with an explanation of what they mean (although it's all pretty obvious):

Make a note. Most of the things you read get stored away in your head somewhere or other. When you see this icon, though, make sure you store this particular item somewhere prominent. It's quite important.

Top Tip. There are lots of ways of saving time, money and effort that you'll never see in print. Except here!

What does it mean? Anything to do with the Internet is packed with jargon. You can't get rid of it, you just have to live with it. But that doesn't mean to say you can't explain it...

#4 Teleworking .net

How to use this book

 Warning! You won't see this icon too often, but when you do, pay attention! Ignoring it could cost you time, money or your sanity. And none of us have much to spare of any of those.

.net Guide

Chapter 1
Introduction

This book is designed to help the potential teleworker get on-line and start telecommuting. It is assumed that the reader has basic computer skills, but is new to using computer-based communications. In this guide, we aim to cut through the seemingly endless sea of jargon that is normally associated with all computer-related activities, to show how being on-line or 'wired' can help the way you work. We will be covering the concept of teleworking in depth, as well as explaining how to go about using telecommunications with a computer and modem.

Subjects such as buying and fitting a modem, using communications software (often referred to as comms software for short) and using the Internet, are explored. Real-world matters are also considered, such as the legalities of using your home for work, tax, insurance and tips on designing a home office. Also included is a Teleworkers Directory, listing useful contacts for associations and groups which specifically help the teleworker, as well as a comprehensive Glossary. You will find Smiley and Acronym Dictionaries that will make sense of the initially confusing net-speak that you may come across when you first get on-line.

Teleworking is an exciting new way of working, and is likely to be used increasingly by all types of businesses in the next few years. It offers benefits for companies, workers, and for the environment. So, what's it all about?

What is teleworking?

Teleworking, in the most basic sense, means to work from home by means of telecommunications. Although this

.net Guide

Introduction

includes relatively simple devices such as the telephone and the fax machine, this book concentrates on using computers and modems with which to do business. Teleworking is seen by many people as being an important new way of working. 'Will Teleworking Work?', a report published by BT in 1994, estimated that by 1995, 2.25 million people will be working from home for more than half of each week.

Modem-equipped computers can transmit any type of computer-held information over a standard telephone line to another suitably equipped machine. Essentially this means that any data file on your machine, be it text, graphics, sound or a mixture of all three, can be transferred to another computer anywhere in the world. You don't have to directly connect to the machine in question though. There are various methods of sending files to a third or intermediator computer, which can act as a sort of storage place or a virtual post office.

In very basic terms, the humble fax machine is just a simple (and relatively slow) modem with an added image scanner to convert printed pages to digital information which can then be transmitted. Received faxes are printed out by an built-in printer after being converted by the modem. Most modems today have fax capabilities built in as standard, and when used in conjunction with a computer, scanner and printer, can offer all the facilities of a fax machine. You could think of a computer with a modem as a sort of souped-up fax machine with a keyboard, screen, sound, go-faster stripes, and fluffy dice. If you did, you might get locked up, but it is one way of visualising what can initially be a confusing and daunting concept.

Why should I want to do it?

Many people would like to work from home rather than in an office. For yourself, it may be because you would enjoy the freedom to set your own working hours, or because you prefer to work alone. Some people prefer to work at times outside the normal 9 to 5 office hours. Many programmers and writers will swear to you that the only sensible time to work is after the witching hour.

It is not, however, a method of working for everybody. Some people find the distractions at home too great, as well as missing the social side of being in an office environment. It can take considerable self-discipline to work from the same place in which you live and some people cannot cope. It can be all too easy to get engrossed in a fascinating documentary about the winter migration of the Albanian Frog on morning television, and think to yourself that you can catch up on work later on – only to get distracted again by something else, thus getting further and further behind. It is strongly recommended that, if practical, a room is set aside as an office specifically for work, so that you can shut out any possible distractions.

For some, however, working at home is the only option. Teleworking can offer people such as the physically disabled, or single parents who are unable to travel to work or to work normal office hours, a way in which to work without needing to leave home. Another big advantage to teleworking, of course, is that you don't have to travel to get to work (walking to the room set aside for working doesn't really count). Not only are you saving your time and money by not being in traffic jams, but you are also helping the environment, albeit in a small way.

 .net Guide

Introduction

By telecommuting, the place in which you live becomes irrelevant. It doesn't matter if you live in the outer Hebrides or on one of the Victorian forts in the middle of the Solent off the Isle of Wight. Teleworking frees you from the inconveniences of having to travel. As someone who hates crossing the sea and who just happens to live on the Isle of Wight (a place not noted for software and book publishing companies), it is the only way to work. Teleworking enables you to live where you want to and not because of where your office is located.

There are numerous benefits to the companies who employ teleworkers too. It cuts down the need to rent expensive office space and reduces overheads such as heat and electricity that go with it. Information can be sent faster and cheaper than by the normal postal method. For example, a document can be sent and be on the client's computer within minutes, instead of the next day. Any changes that need to be made can be re-sent as soon as they are completed. Also, there are no restrictions on sending files on a Sunday, of course!

Being on-line has its own advantages as well. Not only is it a cheaper, faster and more environmentally-friendly way of handling information, but it is, to use a dirty word, FUN! There are literally a million and one things contained within the ever growing global network of computers that is the Internet. Every subject you could ever wish for is covered in some form on the Net – from Scottish country dancing to keeping ferrets. Or a combination of the two. If your job involves any research, the Internet would be a powerful ally.

Who else is doing it?

Teleworking is growing rapidly. Many companies employ teleworkers, or have staff that telecommute for at least part of their working week. Large companies such as British Telecom and Digital have teleworkers as part of their staff, as do smaller companies which may consist entirely of teleworkers and have no offices in the traditional sense. There are numerous associations in existence that are geared to help people telecommute. More are appearing all the time, some in association with the relevant local authority. A selection of these can be found in the Teleworkers Directory located towards the back of the book.

Needless to say, teleworking is only suited to jobs in which the completed work can be transmitted over a telephone line, or where the work uses on-line resources as a tool. This includes obvious occupations such as programmers and journalists, but can also cover a diverse range of workers that includes accountants, market researchers, sales people, telephonists, lawyers and teachers. As technology and the awareness of it increases, so will the number and types of job that will be telecommutable.

Teleworking from home is poised to become an accepted and widespread activity. As businesses become more technology-based, the demand for the flexible, computer-based teleworker will grow.

.net Guide

Chapter 2
Getting Started

To be able to communicate with other computers you need a few basic things:

○ A computer
○ A modem (with a cable or two)
○ Some software
○ A telephone line (with suitable wall socket)

Nothing surprising there, I hope. You may find a printer useful, depending on your type of work, but it is by no means essential to getting on-line.

Welcome to abbreviation land (or **WTAL** as it could be known). It seems that all computer-based activities are littered with daft-looking abbreviations or acronyms. Telecommunications is no different, and indeed is one of the worst culprits for jargonese. All such terms are described when encountered, and there is a completely lovely Glossary at the back to aid you further.

What is a modem?

A modem, which is an abbreviation of MOdulator/DEModulator, is an electronic device that converts computer data into a form that can be transmitted over a standard telephone line. This process is called modulation. The conversion is needed because present telephone lines were designed to transmit the human voice, or sound waves, which are analogue signals. Computers, on the other hand, process information in a series of ones and zeros. This is called binary, and is the language of all modern digital computers.

 .net Guide

Getting Started

In the future, the entire telephone network will undoubtedly become digital, which will make the need for modems redundant. All of the UK's trunk network is already digital, but not all local exchanges are. So, given that, to connect to other computers you must use a modem. But these things aren't like toasters, you need to know a few things before making your choice.

Buying a modem

There are literally dozens of different modems available and it can be very confusing for the first time buyer to know what to look for. Things aren't helped by the modem manufacturers' love of using seemingly meaningless number suffices and abbreviations. Some of these suffices actually mean something, although some may be added to try and make you think that it is the modem equivalent of a Ferrari.

Modems can come with all sorts of lovely sounding features, such as fax send and receive and voice-mail capabilities. But it can all mean nothing if they don't support the correct standards. When it comes to modems, standards are everything.

Here is a breakdown of the letters and numbers that do actually mean something.

The V standards

These indicate which standards the modem supports and have nothing to do with rockets whatsoever. Most are dished out by an organisation called the International Telecommunications Union – Telecommunications or ITU-T. However, not all are universal standards. V.32terbo and V.FC are proprietary standards and were not ratified by the ITU-T, and subsequently are only used by certain manufacturers.

The V standards primarily govern the speed of data transfer and error correction methods, but also include standards for fax transmission. The speed that a modem can transmit data is measured in bits per second (BPS), which should not be confused with the much mis-used term, baud rate. A baud can convey less than or more than one bit of information and was originally used to measure the speed of transmitting Morse code.

BPS (bits per second) is simply the number of bits of information transmitted per second. A byte, or 'character' of information, consists of 8 bits and is used in another term – CPS (characters per second).

Current standards include:

V.17	A fax standard, up to 14400 BPS
V.21	A fax/modem standard, up to 300 BPS
V.22bis	Transfer rate of up to 2400 BPS
V.27ter	A fax standard, up to 4800 BPS
V.29	A fax standard, up to 9600 BPS
V.32bis	Transfer rate up to 14400 BPS
V.32terbo	Transfer rate up to 19200 BPS (proprietary)
V.FC	Transfer rate up to 28800 BPS (proprietary)
V.34	Transfer rate up to 28800 BPS
V.42	Error correction protocol
V.42bis	Data compression protocol

Quite a handful there. Many fast modems, such as V.32bis or V.34 ones, often support some of the lower speed standards as well. These newer models quite often have V.42bis data compression built in, but check the feature list to make sure.

Getting Started 11

Make sure you get a modem with a data compression standard built in, such as V.42bis. This compresses the data as it transfers it, and it can shift up to four times the amount of data than normal. This increased throughput can save you large amounts of time and money. Different types of data compress better than others; relatively simple types such as text compress the best.

To get an idea of the speeds involved, a fifty-page document of 50K (51,200 bytes) in size takes under 36 seconds to transfer using V.32bis and under 18 seconds with a V.34 modem. That doesn't even include data compression, which can reduce transfer times by up to a quarter!

Alas, the standard telephone system has a limited capacity for carrying this sort of data or 'bandwidth' as those in the know call it, and V.34 or its possible 'bis' extension successor, may be one of the last such standards.

Bandwidth is one of the most used terms in telecommunications. In general usage, it describes the amount of data that can go through a particular carrier method, such as a phone line or a fibre-optic cable, at a given rate. These amounts are measured in the usual units, such as bytes/kilobytes, per second. There is now no need to look shocked when you hear someone complaining about the size of their bandwidth.

Other things to know
Another type of standard to look for when choosing a modem is the Hayes command set (also known as the AT

#4 Teleworking .net

command set). This is the de-facto standard for the way modems receive their commands from the computer.

Yet another consideration when buying a modem is that if you intend to connect it to the British Telecom network, it must have British Approvals Board for Telecommunications (BABT) approval. Most modems do have this, and should have a sticker underneath it and on the box to prove it. Any advertisement for a modem must state whether or not it is an approved modem. It is ILLEGAL to use a non-BABT approved modem and if you do, men with pointy sticks may visit your house. But then again they might not.

Modem prices have tumbled recently, and hopefully will continue to do so. Even the fastest, relatively new V.34 models are reasonably priced. So, my general advice would be to buy the fastest modem you can afford, within reason. If you intend spending any serious amount of time on the Internet, or will be transmitting large files, a fast modem will pay for itself in a relatively short time through reduced telephone charges.

For general communications and Internet use, I would suggest nothing slower than V.32bis as these can be had for less than a hundred pounds these days. It may be cheaper to buy a slower modem, but it will cost you more in the long term. If you decide to go for the even faster models, go straight to V.34 and don't bother with V.32terbo or V.FC as these interim standards will ultimately fall by the telecommunications wayside.

If you intend sending or receiving faxes, make sure it has the necessary fax standards. Things to look for here are Class 1 and Class 2 standards. It should also come with, or

 .net Guide

Getting Started

be able to work with, software that is Group III compatible. These are universally-used standards, so there shouldn't be any problems with these. A lot of the newer models have fax capability built in anyway, so essentially you get that feature for free.

But check that the modem supports the standards you know you will need. If your employer, or the on-line service you intend to use, only supports specific standards you need to ensure that your modem has these. There is also little point in splashing out on a fast modem if you will only be using it to connect to a specific place and their modems do not support the same fast standards. Some on-line services, for example, do not currently support speeds greater than V.32bis – so using a V.34 modem on these would be a waste of money.

Inside or out?

With the technical jargon out of the way, another choice has to be made. Modems come in either external or internal flavours. External modems, as the term suggests, are stand-alone devices that sit outside of the computer and are connected to it via a cable. Internal models, spookily enough, need to be installed inside your computer, and therefore do not need a cabled connection. They are generally computer-specific, so you would need to ensure that it is the right one for your system. External modems have their own separate power supplies, whereas internal ones draw their juice from the host computer.

I strongly recommend that you purchase an external modem, as opposed to an internal one. They might cost a few pounds more, but are easier to fit, and will not be

made redundant if you decide to change your computer system in the future.

Cables and things

If you are buying an external modem, you need to make sure you order a RS-232 serial cable to go with it. Unfortunately there is more than one type of serial connector, so you need to check which one your computer has. PCs, for example, may have 9 or 25-pin serial connectors, Amigas have 25-pin and Apple Macs use their own peculiar type. Also check that the cable is wired to support RTS/CTS flow control.

Some modems come bundled with a suitable serial cable, as well as some basic terminal communications software. Fax modems may also come with some sort of fax software as well, which you will need to be able to send and receive faxes. But be sure to check that the software will work with your computer system. Shop around for the best deals!

The other cable you will need is the one that connects the modem to the phone wall socket. This should come with the modem, so hopefully you won't need to worry about getting one. If for some reason there isn't one included with your modem, run along to the nearest phone shop (with your modem) and they should be able to sort you out.

Modem checklist

A quick round-up of what you need to remember when buying a modem:

 .net Guide

Getting Started   15

- Make sure it supports the required V standards – Check if you need it to talk to a particular type of modem, or standard.

- Make sure it has data compression such as V.42bis

- That it is Hayes or AT command set compatible

- Check that it can send and receive faxes, if you require it

- If you are buying an external modem, you will need a serial cable

Once the deed has been done and you have that shiny new modem, the time comes to start doing things with it. First the computer and modem must be joined, in holy telewedlock.

Installing a modem

Now we get to the nitty-gritty. Time to get those hands dirty!

Before getting involved in installing your modem, make sure there is a phone jack in reaching distance of your computer. If there isn't one close enough, you can either get an additional wall socket kit and install that, or you can cheat like me and get a phone cable extension lead. Both should be available from your local friendly telephone emporium.

#4 Teleworking .net

Connecting a modem to your computer should be very straightforward, especially if you have an external model. You should always read the instructions supplied with the modem before doing anything and have them to hand whilst on the job.

If you have opted for an internal modem, this will mean you will have the seemingly scary task of taking the cover off your computer to install it. But don't panic! As long as you take your time and follow the instructions, things should go swimmingly.

Whenever installing any piece of hardware inside your computer, make sure you have plenty of elbow room. If possible, place the computer somewhere free of junk, like a nice clear desk, and have everything you need close to hand. Make a cup of coffee (but keep it away from the equipment!), take your time, follow the instructions to the letter. Stay calm. DON'T be like me and try to install hardware in a broom cupboard, against the stopwatch and whilst playing the banjo.

IMPORTANT! Observe any static precautions in the installation instructions! Static can do very nasty things to computer components, so discharge any static from yourself by grounding yourself, or by wearing an anti-static wristband. Tying your head to a radiator may be considered overdoing things a bit!

Ensure that your computer has been disconnected from the mains socket before removing the cover. Make certain that the slot or pins are properly lined up before pushing the

.net Guide

Getting Started 17

modem card in. Do not push too hard, or you may damage some tracks or pins. If you have trouble getting the card in, try gently wiggling it into place. Whatever you do, don't resort to using a hammer, however tempting it gets.

Hopefully your hardware is now ready for action, so to speak. But before you can get connected to anywhere, you will need some software to make the modem do useful things...

What Software do I need?

It all depends on what sort of communicating you need to do. For basic comms operations such as direct modem to modem transfers and calling an on-line service or BBS, you need some terminal software (which also goes under the generic term of communications or comms software). This will enable you to send commands to the modem, and to send and receive files, at the very least. There is a wide choice of terminal programs for just about every personal computer under the sun, costing from nothing to several hundred pounds. They vary wildly in features: some are very basic, having only the barest of features, whereas some offer high-end capabilities such as built-in electronic conferencing or the ability to act as a BBS.

Things to look for in a comms program include:

○ review buffer (stores the information that is displayed whilst on-line)

○ support for a wide variety of transfer protocols (such as Zmodem, Ymodem etc.)

#4 Teleworking .net

Chapter 2

Smartcom for Windows is a popular comms program.

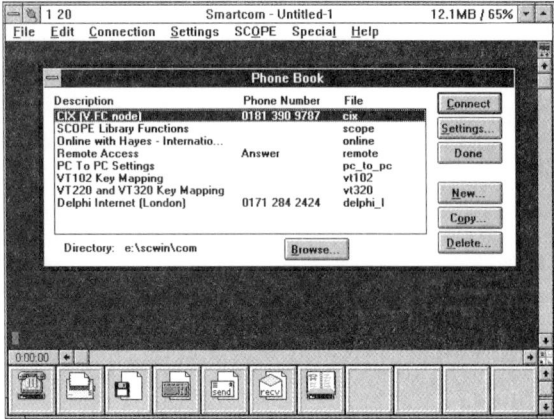

○ a host mode capability (lets people ring-up and connect to your machine)

○ a phone book feature (saves tedious dialling by hand)

○ script or macro facility (enables you to automate your connections)

For faxing, you need some software to enable the modem to prepare and send outgoing faxes and to receive and display incoming ones. Once a fax is received it can be stored on the hard drive as a graphical image, or it can be printed out. The fax graphic images can take up quite a lot of disk space, especially if you receive faxes regularly – so they are best deleted after you print them out, unless you need to keep them for future reference.

Many fax modems are supplied with simple fax packages or 'lite' versions of bigger, commercial ones. For occasional use these would probably suffice, but there are a selection of feature-rich commercial packages available for most popular computers. Some of the more expensive offerings include

Getting Started 19

Optical Character Recognition (OCR) capability. This process can (with wildly varying degrees of success) take a received fax image and extract the text from it, by converting it into the more flexible form of ASCII text. This enables you to store the fax content in a much smaller form, and gives you the option of editing it or including pieces of it into other documents.

If you plan on accessing the Internet via an on-line service such as Cix or Delphi, then all you need is the basic terminal software mentioned above. However, if you intend having a direct Internet connection, then the type of software you need becomes a little more involved. It depends on the sort of features you intend to use and is discussed in the Internet chapter.

Using a modem

Once everything is connected together, we can begin to delve into the black art of computer 'comms. So with pointy hat (silver stars are optional) and flowing robe carefully donned, we must now learn the chants that will make the modem manifest into being and perform great acts of magic.

Well, okay, it's not quite like that. You can still wear the hat and the robe though – I do. But before we get down to serious spell-weaving, you have to configure your comms software...

Setting up your comms software

The most basic piece of software you will need for telecommuting is the terminal or comms program. These

Chapter 2

come in a variety of guises, from the very simple to do-everything packages which can cost several hundred pounds. At the very least, a comms program will be able to let you dial another modem, connect to it and enable you to send and receive files from the attached computers.

Before you can use the software, you will need to configure it. Some of the smarter packages (like Smartcom for Windows) will ask you to choose your particular modem model from a list, as part of their installation. If your modem is on the list, then selecting it will (hopefully) enable the software to fully or partially auto-configure itself. Don't worry if your modem isn't on the list (which is likely if the software is of American origin) – just pick the one that says 'any modem' or 'generic'.

Assuming that you need to hand-configure the various settings, here follows a breakdown of the basic items that need to be set-up. Even if the software appears to have done the job for you, it is worthwhile understanding the terms used as it is likely you will need to modify them now and again.

Serial port location Some computers, for example PCs, may have more than one serial port. You need to tell the comms program which one the modem is connected to.

Baud rate setting Also referred to as transmission rate, serial port speed, or DTE (Data Terminal Equipment) speed. This is used to describe the speed at which the computer and modem talk to each other. If you have data compression built into your modem, such as V.42bis, you need to have this set to at least two or three times the BPS speed of your modem. For example, you would set a

 .net Guide

Getting Started 21

V.32bis modem with V.42bis compression at 38400 – rather than the 14400 BPS speed of V.32bis. Setting it at a lower value could slow down transfer speeds and increase your time on the phone.

Data bits/Parity/Stop bits Together, these three terms describe the format of each character of information that the computer will send to the modem. They need to be set the same as the computer you are calling. If they aren't, you will end up with a screenful of garbage. Their settings are often shown together, separated by hyphens – in the form: data bits – parity – stop bits. An example being 8-N-1, which tells us that there are eight data bits, no parity and one stop bit. 8-N-1 is by far the most common, although some systems may use 7-E-1 settings.

Flow control This is a technique used by a modem to monitor the amount of data coming from the computer or other modem. You should have this set to RTS/CTS if your cable supports it, otherwise use XON/XOFF.

There may well be a lot more options or settings in your comms software, but those above cover the essentials. You can always go back and modify the others when you are more familiar with the program. If in doubt, leave the setting at the default value!

You should now be ready for some action. It could be a good idea to test that everything is properly connected before going further...

#4 Teleworking **.net** *the internet magazine*

Making sure it all works

Now all that funny business is out of the way, we come to making sure that everything works as it is meant to.

What follows is just a simple test to try and verify that all the connections are correct and that the modem is receiving its commands from the computer properly. As computer systems vary wildly, it is impossible to cover any little quirks your particular set-up might throw at you. But unless you are very unlucky, this test should work without a glitch.

Firstly, check that all connections appear okay, then switch on the computer and modem. You then need to load the terminal software, making sure you have set it up for your modem.

Once loaded, you should be presented with an empty, or near empty screen, into which you can type things.

Try typing the following: `PLEASE CONNECT ME TO THE INTERNET <return>`

What?!? It didn't work? I'm afraid things aren't quite that simple yet – maybe in a few years' time. Let's try using some real commands.

`ATZ <return>`

The modem should have responded with an 'OK' message after a brief pause. 'ATZ' is a command from the Hayes command set, which mostly start with the prefix 'AT'. What this command does is to reset the modem, so that it reverts back to the settings it had when you first switched it on.

 .net Guide

Getting Started   **23**

If it didn't work as expected, you need to make sure that all cable connections are secure. Also, check that your comms program is set up correctly and knows such things as which port your modem is connected to on your computer.

If everything appears fine and dandy, we can get down to some real business.

Hayes/AT commands

The modem is essentially a dumb box which can't do anything useful until it is told to by the computer. For nearly all modems, these instructions are called the Hayes or AT command set.

To enter these commands, you need to load your comms program and have it set up as described above. If you are presented with a choice, make sure the program is in 'terminal mode'. Eventually, you should be presented with a screen into which you can type.

From here, you can enter the AT commands that control your modem. There are quite a few commands – but you only need to know a few to get by. To use a command, you must start with the 'AT' prefix, and enter type in either lower or upper-case – not a mixture of the two.

Some commonly used AT commands are:

AT   ATtention! (Goes before any command)
D<n>   Dial command, followed by number to dial
H<0 or 1> 0 – Hang up phone, 1 – Go off hook

#4 Teleworking

Chapter 2

The ATI4 command returns the settings of my modem.

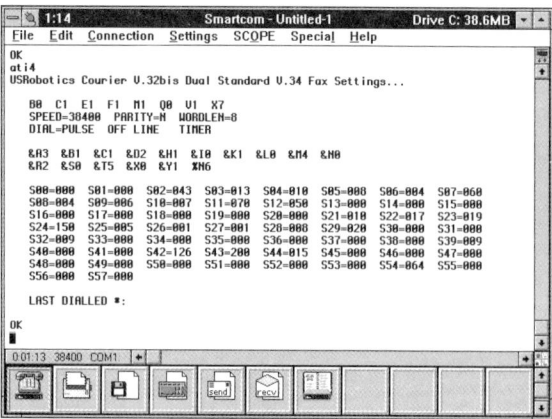

I\<n\>		Inquiry – returns information about your modem

M\<n\>		Monitor speaker (0 – speaker off, 1 – speaker on)

S\<n\> = \<x\>	Sets S-register \<n\> to value \<x (between 0-255)\>

Z		Modem reset

If you don't specify a number, the value is assumed to be 0. S-registers control the internal features of modems and are used for fine-tuning the way it operates. You normally don't have to bother touching these, but a full list of the functions available should be listed in your manual.

For example, you would use the commands 'ATH0' (or just 'ATH') to hang-up the phone line and 'ATM1' to turn the speaker on.

Commands can be added one after another, on the same line. You only need to use one 'AT' at the start, which then signals to the modem that a command, or multiple commands follow. For example, 'AT Z DT 123456' – this

 .net Guide

Getting Started 25

tells the modem to reset itself, then dial the number '123456'. Note that the spaces between the commands are optional.

Dialling and connecting

Now we come to the important bit – how to dial and connect to another modem.

The command for dialling a number, as mentioned previously, is 'ATD' (including the 'AT' prefix). There are several sub-commands for the dialling command, one of which is 'T' which stands for Tone dial.

Thus the command for dialling a normal phone number is: 'ATDT <number>' followed by <return>.

After dialling the number, you should hear a short ringing tone through the modem's speaker (unless it is engaged, in which case you need to try again). The modem at the other end should then answer, and you should be treated to a high-pitched whistling sound. This is the sound of the modems introducing themselves to each other. They are finding out what speeds and protocols the other supports, and agreeing on using the ones that both have.

After a few seconds of this, you should hopefully be greeted with a connect string – which looks something like this:

CONNECT 14400/ARQ/V32/LAPM/V42BIS

This tells us at what speed the modems have connected and if data compression is enabled. It will, of course, vary depending on your modem, or the modem that you are talking to.

If for some reason the phone line is dropped by the other modem, or if there is some fault – the connection may be halted and the modem will respond with the message, 'NO CARRIER'. This means that the modem can no longer detect the carrier signal and thus has hung-up the 'line.

Sending and receiving files

Once you are connected to another modem, you need to know how to go about transferring your files. This process, called uploading or downloading a file, should be very straightforward. Depending on your comms software, the receiving part of a transfer may be automatic. The sending of a file normally only requires a choice of which transfer method or protocol to use, and the selection of the file to send from your computer.

Uploading is the term used for sending a file, and downloading for when you receive a file. A way to remember it is to think of the data flowing 'up' the cable when you send something, or 'down' it when receiving!

Transfer protocols

In order to send or receive data – to or from a file – you need to use something called a transfer protocol. This enables the comms program to know when a file transfer starts and ends, as well as the size of the transfer. Most protocols also send the name of the file beforehand, so that the receiving computer knows what to call it. They also offer

 .net Guide

Getting Started

extra error checking, so that you know the file being sent will arrive intact at its destination.

Most comms programs enable you to choose a default protocol. This is the protocol that the software will use for transfers, unless you tell it otherwise. A lot of programs can also auto-detect an incoming file transfer. When they sense that a file is being received, they can start the downloading without you having to do anything.

There are quite a few types of transfer protocols available, each different in how they transmit the data.

Three of the most commonly used protocols are Xmodem, Ymodem and Zmodem.

Of the three, the most used and probably best protocol for fast (over 2400 BPS) transfers is Zmodem. It is recommended that you use this protocol when available, or Ymodem if it is not. Xmodem should only be used if the others are not available, as it is a relatively inefficient transfer method.

Direct file transfers

The simplest form of teleworking with a modem is the direct modem to modem transfer. With this, you can use your modem to directly call the computer that you wish to send the file to, without going through a third-party system. By using this method, the only cost is the price of the telephone call.

The most basic way of doing this is to have comms software loaded on both machines – and having the computer that is going to receive the file in auto-answer mode.

WHAT DOES IT MEAN? Auto-answer mode simply makes the modem listen out for a call, and then answers it when someone rings. The command 'AT S0 = 1' should put your modem into answer mode.

All you then need to do is dial the number of that computer, and after connection start the upload file procedure. The comms software on the receiving computer may handle the auto-detection of file transfers – otherwise a human will have to tell it to download the file. If auto-detection is not available, it would be a good idea to confirm the filename and protocol method you will be using with the person in question beforehand. You can do this either by the good old-fashioned voice phone call – or by chatting whilst on-line, which you can do simply by typing the messages on the keyboard.

This method of file transfer is very crude, and is not recommended. It may serve you if you have no other option, or if you need to use it in an emergency.

Another, more elegant way of transferring files with direct modem to modem transfers, is for one of the computers to go into something called host mode...

Being a good host

The 'host mode' feature provides a friendly front-end for direct modem to modem file transfers. Entering this mode places the modem into auto-answer mode, ready for the sender to call you. After the other modem has rung and the connection is established, the computer in host mode presents the caller with a mini-BBS type menu. This can give the caller the option of uploading or downloading a file, or

.net .net Guide

Getting Started 29

leaving a message for the person at the other end. The features available obviously vary from package to package, but the basic ability to receive unattended transfers or messages is the main thing.

This is obviously only useful if someone calls you – or if their comms software supports host mode.

Chapter 3
The Internet

The Internet. You can't have failed to have seen it in the news, or read about it in all sorts of places, from What Knitting? to computer magazines. It has been hailed by some as the greatest telecommunications system yet developed, and by others as just a computer-based CB radio-like fad. It has certainly generated a lot of interest from end-users to the biggest multi-national companies. But, what is it and will it bite?

It won't bite me, will it?

The Internet is, very simply, a global network of interconnected computer networks. The networks that together form the Net (as it is also known) vary, from the likes of large US Government organisations, university and college networks, billion-dollar corporations such as IBM, commercial on-line services such as Delphi, Cix and CompuServe, down to individual personal machines. From its humble origins it has grown to a huge sprawling system that covers most of the countries on the planet. But it is very hard to measure accurately the size of the Internet, as there is no single registry, or directory, like there is with the telephone network. But some estimates say that there are as many as 30 million people with Internet access, using something like 3 million computers, and it continues to grow daily at a phenomenal rate.

MAKE A NOTE! **The Internet probably contains the highest density of abbreviations and acronyms than anywhere else. Don't let the weird looking 'words' put you off. Make good use of the Acronym Dictionary at the back. Be warned though – never, ever ask anyone on the Net what a FAQ is! (Go on, look it up.)**

The Internet is a very strange creature. As nobody ever sat down and planned its development, it is the product of evolution rather than a grand design. Although it is a relatively recent development, its roots go back over twenty-five years.

A brief history

Back in the technological stone ages, in 1969, a small yet important event happened that was to result in the wonderful beast we have today. Yes, that's right, it was the year I was born. Coincidentally, it was also the year the Internet was conceived, albeit unintentionally (hey, that's something else we share). Under the control of the US Government's Advanced Research Projects Agency, it started life as a small secure network, which was named ARPANET after the Agency. It originally comprised of just four supercomputers which were housed at various places in the US. ARPANET was designed as a robust network having no central authority, as each computer on the network had equal status. This idea, which would later be an essential key in its growth into the Internet, was so that ARPANET could continue to function even if parts of it were destroyed by a nuclear attack.

As the four computers were connected on dedicated high-speed links, scientists and researchers could share one another's computer facilities remotely – a sort of very early form of teleworking. By 1972, ARPANET had grown to some thirty-seven computers and something odd was starting to happen. It soon become apparent that the network was being used for things other than research and computer sharing. Users had created their own personal electronic mailboxes and were swapping messages, firstly about their work, but soon just idle chat. It wasn't long before mailing-lists were invented, where an identical message could be broadcast to large numbers of network users. This was frowned upon as it wasn't 'work', but it happened anyway.

Throughout the 1970s ARPANET grew steadily, but remained tightly controlled. But in 1983, the military segment, possibly concerned with security, broke off to form MILNET. A turning-point for the Internet came the next year, 1984, when the National Science Foundation (another United States Government Agency) established NSFNET. This consisted of five supercomputer centres, more powerful than the original ARPANET systems, located in different regions of the United States. Initially it was set up as a network for educational facilities, so that they could use the supercomputing power for academic research. However, as with ARPANET, it was soon being used for things other than pure research and it wasn't long before the system was feeling the strain.

In 1987, NSFNET underwent a massive overhaul that resulted in yet faster computers and network links. This was to herald an explosion in growth. NASA joined, as did the US Department of Energy, followed by many others. Soon after, the Internet, as it had come to be known, was opened to other countries' academic facilities – provided that they were allies of the United States. During the early 1990s, the floodgates were well and truly thrown open, and the Internet was made accessible to anyone who could connect to it.

What use is it to me?

The Internet is potentially the most useful communications system yet developed. With it you can send and receive mail messages and data files to and from any other Internet-connected computer on the planet, without running up telephone number-sized phone bills. To connect, you dial to an Internet service whose machines are permanently connected to the Internet. Depending on where you live, this can be just a local call. In this way, your work can be transmitted over a telephone line much faster and often cheaper than conventional transport-based delivery methods.

Not only is it a powerful data transport method, but it is also a huge information resource. Depending on your type of work, the chances are you will find information useful to your business. The benefits to a computer-based job are obvious, as the Internet has a staggering amount of computer-related information, as you would expect. But virtually every other profession is catered for on the Net, in one way or another. If your job requires that you need to research certain subjects, it is likely that the Internet will prove itself to be an excellent reservoir of information. Being connected to the Net is like having access to the largest library in the world, and all from the comfort of your own home!

There is also a huge amount of free or shareware software available for downloading – literally billions of bytes worth. Just about every type of program you could imagine, for a wide range of personal computers, is catered for. Many software publishers put updates or patches to their programs on the Net, as well as other useful files or information.

#4 Teleworking the internet magazine .net

36   Chapter 3

Aided by the recent development of the World Wide Web (covered later in this Chapter) the commercialisation of the Internet is gathering pace. What this will eventually result in is anyone's guess, but it will see many thousands of companies, big and small, connecting to, and doing business on the Net. By being on the Internet, you would be in a position to offer these companies your services, by contacting them directly or through advertising. But be warned, advertising on the Internet is a thorny subject to say the least, so tread very carefully. It would probably be best to advertise yourself using the World Wide Web, by having your own Web page; or by offering your services inside an on-line service such as Cix. Whatever you do, do not advertise willy-nilly on Usenet. People have been mail-bombed for this, as it is frowned upon by the majority of Internet users who perceive the Net as a 'pure' information system which should not be commercialised in any way.

Mail-bombing is when thousands of irate Internet users email some poor sap with a load of electronic junk, thus clogging up their mailbox. The recipient will have to spend more time on-line downloading it all, thus costing more in telephone charges. They might also lose important email in the deluge or, if their system can't cope, it might even cause a computer crash. Blatant advertising in the wrong place will guarantee you this action. Best not to try.

The amazing thing about the Internet is that it can do so much, but cost so little. If you use an Internet provider service, such as Demon, you may only be charged a fixed flat-rate per month. You are not charged any extra at all for the type or amount of things you do whilst on the Net,

.net Guide

The Internet

other than your telephone charges (which, if you are suitably located, will be at local call rates). Some services charge for the amount of time you use and can be economical if you only intend to use the Net occasionally.

Before we explore what the Internet can do for you, it is worth explaining how the machines on the Net use addresses – so you won't be frightened when you see things like '`spooky.demon.co.uk`'...

Internet addresses

Every machine on the Net has a unique address, so that the rest of the computers on the Internet know where to find it. These are made up of a series of numbers separated by dots, and are called IP addresses, an example being: 158.152.82.60. Luckily, you don't have to bother with these numbers, as you can use the site name of the machine or network instead.

A site name is the unique name given to a computer or network on the Net. It is also referred to as the server name, node name, or the domain. Together the codes may tell you what type of service it provides, who operates it, and where it is.

Site names are comprised of two or more letter-based codes, separated by dots. For example, the name of my Demon domain is '`spooky.demon.co.uk`'. Reading it backwards, the last code is called the top level domain and can either refer to the country the node is in, or the type of organisation that operates it. Generally, nodes in the United

#4 Teleworking .net

States don't normally have a country code (I guess as they started it, they can do what they like).

Examples of other countries' codes are:

au   Australia
de   Germany
fr   France
ie   Ireland
jp   Japan
ru   Russian Federation
us   United States

Still reading backwards, next to the top level domain, are parts that specify the organisation type, their name and the hostname. The 'co' part tells us that the node is operated by a commercial service; 'demon' is the name of the company running the service; and 'spooky' is the name I chose for my hostname. If the last part of the address isn't a country code, then it denotes what kind of body runs it.

Other top level domain codes:

com   Commercial organisation
edu   Educational facility
gov   Government body
mil   Military node
org   Other organisations
net   Network resources

An example of a commercial company's domain is 'microsoft.com'. This, of course, belongs to Microsoft who are indeed a commercial concern.

The Internet 39

If the node is dedicated to a particular service, like the World Wide Web or FTP, then they usually (but not always) start with a code which shows this. For example, the name of the FTP server at Demon is called '`ftp.demon.co.uk`'.

Other codes include:

archie	Node is an Archie server
gopher	Node is a Gopher server
telnet	You can Telnet to this machine
www	This is a Web site

Don't worry if these terms mean nothing to you yet – they will be covered later on.

If you are unsure of the exact name of a company's FTP or Web server, you can have a good guess. For example, we know that 'microsoft.com' belongs to Microsoft Software, so you could add 'ftp' to the front of it, to get 'ftp.microsoft.com' – which could then be the name of their FTP server. Which it is!

Here follows a compact guide to the aspects of the Internet you are most likely to find useful when telecommuting. For a more detailed look into the Net, you might like to check out the parent book to this series, 'All you need to know about The Internet' by the well-known Net-Hipster, Davey Winder. Details are at the end of this guide.

Electronic mail

Electronic mail, or email for short, is probably the most useful and indeed most used tool of the Internet. With it, not only can you send and receive mail or files to and from any other email address on the Internet, but you can also use it to subscribe to mailing lists, amongst other things. It is very fast, many times quicker than normal 'snail-mail'. You could send an email message to someone in America and it could be sitting in their mailbox, ready for them to read, within a minute or two.

WHAT DOES IT MEAN

Regular mail delivery methods such as the Royal Mail are called 'snail-mail' as they are so much slower than email!

Not only is email faster than normal letter post, but it is also more economical. On the Internet, you are not charged any extra for sending mail. It makes no difference if you are emailing someone down the road, or someone in Japan, cost-wise. Also you don't need to be on-line when some email is sent to you in order to receive it. When mail for you is received by your Internet provider, it is stored on one of their computers, ready for you to collect it when you next log on. So, by having an email address, you have a 24-hour, 7 days a week contact point.

Just having an email address can look good for your business. There is a certain amount of kudos to be had by having an electronic mail address on your business stationery. It shows prospective clients that you are on the Net and are using the latest communications technology. As the Internet revolution thunders onward, it will make sense for businesses to communicate using electronic mail. Not only will it save greatly on postage costs, but it will increase the speed of doing business. A few simple mail exchanges with your client via Royal Mail could take as much as a week. With the Internet-based email, it would be possible to do the same thing in an hour. But what makes up an email address, and what does one look like?

Email addresses

Just like the plain, old-fashioned 'snail mail', email needs to be addressed properly in order to get to its destination. Electronic mail addresses are much more compact than normal postal addresses. Instead of having the road and town details, you use the name or address of the computer on which the mailbox lives. They take the form of:

`username@sitename`

The '`username`' part is quite obvious, I hope. It is used to specify your personal mailbox on the system that you use. The '`@`' symbol means just that – so an address could be read as '`username`' at '`sitename`'. For example, one of my email addresses is:

`simon@spooky.demon.co.uk`

'`simon`' is, wait for it, my given name and '`spooky`' is the name I chose for my domain. '`demon`' is the name of the Internet provider, and the '`co.uk`' tells us that they are a commercial company based in the UK. Easy, really.

> **TOP TIP**
> If you are unsure of a user's name, but have the rest of the email address, you can try mailing the postmaster at that address and asking politely for help. For example, for my domain name you would mail postmaster@spooky.demon.co.uk.

Some direct Internet service providers, such as Demon, let you choose the name of your domain. For an email account that is to be used for business, you should bear in mind the impression the name will give to prospective clients. For example, using the domain name 'hopeless', which could result in an email address such as `apathetic@hopeless.demon.co.uk`, might not inspire confidence in some quarters.

Even if you do not have the option of choosing your domain name, you still have to consider what username you wish to go under. Choose carefully, as not all systems will allow you to change usernames easily. It is always a good idea to pick a memorable username or domain name for your email address. A safe bet is to use your business name, which obviously makes everything look neat on your letterheads. As well as being easily recognisable for your clients, it could also be used as a subtle form of advertising when you post a message in a Usenet newsgroup, or in a conference inside an on-line service.

Using email

Electronic mail is quite different from your regular, old-fashioned snail-mail. People are almost always less formal in their email, even large businesses. This will take some getting used to, if you are used to writing the standard formal letter. You will find that email messages are generally more compact, and get to the point quickly. For example:

```
John,

Please find enclosed the updated files
(attached at the bottom of this mail). All
changes are listed in the CHANGES.TXT file.
Let me know if you have problems.

Regards, Simon.
```

It's a weird effect, but somehow email makes most people more chummy. It certainly makes for a friendly and less stuffy way of communicating. But it is best to use a fairly formal tone when emailing someone for the first time, until you have an idea of their style – or until you get to know them better. As in that thing they call real-life, not everyone is the same.

When you send some email, you also have to supply a subject title to go with it. This should have some meaning, so that when the receiver looks at their mailbox, they have an idea as to the content of the mail. When replying to email, a lot of mail packages append 'Re:' to the subject title. This, as you would expect, means 'in reference to'. It also helps to keep track of which mail message is in reply to another.

You might be thinking that this email business sounds rather useful. But however tempting it might be, given that it can be essentially free or at worst, very cheap, it is generally not a good idea to use email for mailshots, or advertising in any form. Mass mailshots are a no-no. If by chance you email the wrong people, you may find yourself the victim of a mail-bombing campaign which is the on-line equivalent of a mass mob throwing rocks through your windows.

Having said that, the odd mail to selected businesses, touting for work, may be ok. But make sure your email is targeted at the right person, and include some form of advance apology for any offence or inconvenience. Something like 'Please accept my apologies for any inconvenience this message may have caused you, if this mail is not of interest' at the end would be a good idea. People can get quite offended by receiving this sort of mail as they are paying phone and possibly on-line charges to read it. It is best limited to company mailboxes, who are more likely to be interested in your services.

Sending and receiving files

The sending and receiving of your computer files is quite likely to be one of your most important on-line activities. There are several ways of sending and receiving files via the Internet. One of the simplest ways is via electronic mail. This is not limited to simple text messages as you might think, but can be used for transporting all types of computer data, and a whole lot more besides.

Another way to move your files over the Net is to use the FTP facility. This is more likely to be used if you are dealing with a company which has their own direct, permanent connection to the Internet, or if you need to move large amounts of data. It is also the Internet's standard way of transporting files, and can be used to obtain software or information files useful to your work. Let's look at both features in turn.

Sending files via email

Rather than just being limited to sending text-only mail messages, email can be used to transport all types of file to any other email address on the planet. If the file you need to send just consists of ASCII text, then you have no problem, as you send it as you would any other email message. However, if you need to send more complex data, such as a graphic or spreadsheet file, then another method is needed. This is because ASCII, and therefore email, can only send 7-bit character values – whereas data normally consists of 8-bits per character. So a way is needed to fit this digital quart into a virtual pint pot.

One way of sending a binary file is to use a process called UUencoding. This process converts the 8-bit values needed into the 7-bit ones, by 'stretching' out the characters. Where it would normally take 56-bits of information to store 7 bytes of characters, when UUencoded, it takes 8 characters. If you are using large files, this could make the resulting email message very large – and a lot of mail packages or systems have a limit on the size of an individual message. To get round this, the UUencoder program can split a file across several email messages.

The reverse process of this is called, unsurprisingly, UUdecoding. This takes the email message or messages which contain the UUencoded information and rebuilds the file for you. There are various programs that handle both the encoding and decoding for you, and some mail programs have this built in which makes it a lot easier.

UUencoding is not the only way you can send files via electronic mail. There is another, more recent development called Multi-purpose Internet Mail Extensions (or MIME for short). This is a standard for adding binary files to your email. It can attach any type of file – pictures, sounds, spreadsheet data, whatever – to your text messages. Not all mail programs can handle MIME yet, so you would need to check that your package, as well as the person you would be sending it to does support it.

Some MIME mail programs also have the ability to display any attached multimedia file from the received MIME-mail, as well as saving it as a file on your hard drive. Therefore, you could email someone to explain the benefits of your new service and add a picture of something to illustrate it. They would then see the picture whilst reading your message, giving your sales-pitch maximum effect!

Transferring files using FTP

FTP stands for File Transfer Protocol, which is the standard system for moving files on the Internet. With it, you can send or receive files to or from a machine on the Internet. You can't just connect to any old machine on the Net, though. It has to be an FTP server, and its address will usually (but not always) start with the 'ftp' code. For example, Demon Internet's FTP server is `ftp.demon.co.uk`. There are a lot of FTP sites located all over the globe, certainly more than you could shake a stick at. Not

The Internet

FTP in action!

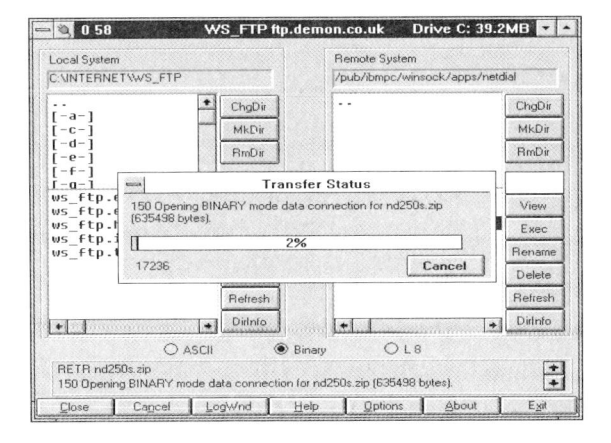

all FTP servers are open to everyone though. Publicly accessible ones are called Anonymous FTP servers, as you log-in using 'anonymous' as your name. Some of the commercial companies' sites, such as Microsoft's, contain only software connected to their products. But most are big collecting pots for all sorts of wonders.

FTP is one of the most-used features of the Net, after email. However, you are unlikely to use FTP to transfer your own files, unless you or your client has a dedicated FTP server permanently connected to the Net. This is because, unlike email, FTP requires that you are directly linked to the machine in question. It is possible for you to set your machine to act as an FTP server whilst you are on-line, but this takes quite a bit of effort. You would also have to pre-arrange a time for you and the recipient to be on-line. In my own humblest of opinions, it is far easier to use email to transport your files.

What you are most likely to use FTP for, however, is getting software and information files – of which there is a staggering amount – from around the Net . If you use or

#4 Teleworking .net

intend to use a computer for your business, there is sure to be some software out there that can make your life easier, and probably save you money as well. Just about every type of program you can imagine is available for downloading off the Net. From word processors, powerful databases, spreadsheets to art programs – it's all there. A lot of it is also free; all you need to do is download it and it's yours to keep. However, some of the software is shareware, which means that you can evaluate the software for a specified period, after which if you want to keep using it you are morally obliged to pay to have it 'registered'.

When you register a shareware program, you may be sent a printed manual, be entitled to an improved version, or be sent updates when they become available. It varies from program to program – but at the very least you get the satisfaction of having done the right thing. For some authors, this is their business and they depend on people being honest in order for them to pay the rent.

To be able to get your hands on this mountain of binary goodies, you need to connect to the FTP server in question. The exact way you do this depends on your Internet connection, and the software you use. When you get to the log-in prompt, you need to type '`anonymous`'. After that you will be asked for a password, which is your email address.

When you type in your email address as the password, you don't have to type the whole thing. As the FTP computer knows the name of the Internet service you are calling from, you only need to type 'username@', followed by return. For example, instead of typing 'simon@spooky.demon.co.uk', I can just type 'simon@'.

The Internet

Archie makes finding files easy.

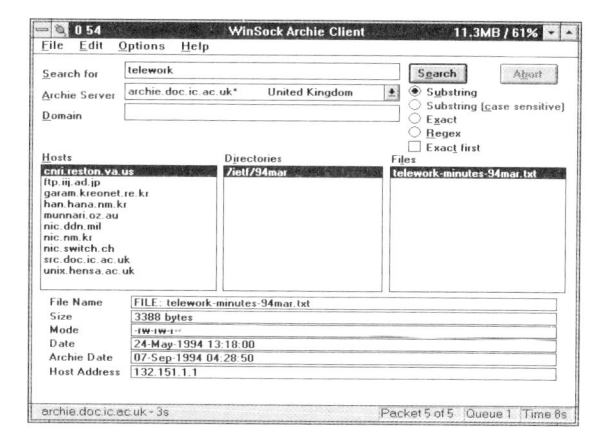

Once you have logged on, you will probably need to go into the PUB directory, inside which is the public accessible software. In here you will find all sorts of directory headings, and lots of files inside them. You can easily find yourself downloading huge amounts of software that you might not actually need, so it's a good idea to know what you are after before you go FTPing. You can also get files from FTP servers via email – there are details in the On-Line Resources section at the back of this guide.

Searching for files with Archie

To help you locate a particular file or document on many of the vast arrays of FTP sites around the world, there is a search tool called Archie. This will search a huge number of FTP sites for you, and return the locations of any matching files it finds. It can search for the whole filename, or just part of it. To use this tool, you need to connect to an Archie server, in a similar way you connect to other types of servers (FTP, WWW etc.) with a program called an Archie client. You can also use it via the World Wide Web or from within

Gopher. This is an invaluable tool for locating files whose names you at least have an idea of. It can also be useful for locating files on specific subjects (as long as the file has part of it in the name).

Information on the Net

Information is primarily what the Internet is all about. There is a mind-boggling amount of information on just about every subject you could wish for. It is not simply limited to computer-related topics – a wide spectrum of subjects are covered. Virtually all the research for this humble tome was done on-line. This being a book concerned with getting on-line and using it, that is hardly surprising. But I should emphasise that the information available is not exclusively for wire-heads. However specialised or unique your business may be, there is almost certainly material of interest to you, sitting on the Net, somewhere.

Mailing lists

Mailing lists are discussion groups on specific subjects that are distributed via email. There are thousands of different lists, covering a wide range of topics including at least one especially for teleworkers (see the Teleworkers Directory at the back). To join or 'subscribe to' a mailing-list, you have to mail a particular email address requesting that you be added. This is normally achieved by a simple command in either the email subject heading, or in the body of the message. Sometimes, all you need to do is simply send some blank email and you will be joined automatically. The exact method of subscribing varies from list to list. Once joined, you will receive all that is posted to the mailing-list via your personal email. The amount and regularity of the postings depends on how many people post to that list.

To post a message of your own to the list, you normally only need to reply to any one of the mailings or you might have to mail another, different address. Some mailing-lists, especially those for news or announcements are 'read-only' and cannot be posted to directly.

Mailing-lists are generally information-dense, that is to say that not a lot of waffle goes on – unlike some parts of Usenet. Talking of Usenet...

Usenet

Usenet is a huge, globally-distributed discussion system. Like conferences or forums found in on-line systems such as Cix or Delphi, it is organised into different subject headings – called newsgroups (or just 'groups'). People post messages or 'articles' to these newsgroups using the appropriate software. These articles are then 'broadcast' to all interconnected computers, not just the Internet. The Net is just one of the various networks that carry Usenet traffic. There are a vast number of Usenet newsgroups, covering many subjects. Currently there are over 10,000 such groups, and more are created daily.

Most Internet service providers and on-line services offer a full Usenet service, so you can join (or 'subscribe to' as it is also known) to any group that takes your fancy. But some services restrict or censor certain newsgroups (such as the sex-based ones) from their Usenet 'feed'.

Some of these newsgroup are 'moderated', and articles to such groups must first be mailed to the 'moderator' for approval before they are posted. Most newsgroups are not moderated, so you can post directly to them. But when posting an article, you should be aware of the huge number of people that are going to be reading it. Many groups can have readerships measured in the hundreds of thousands – so you need to be careful about what you post. Don't post overlong messages, or do things like quoting a large previous message, only to put 'I agree' at the bottom. Lots of people could download and read your message, so it's worth pausing to make sure it is suitable.

The first thing to do when joining a newsgroup is to read the FAQ (Frequently Asked Questions) file for that group. These are sometimes periodically posted in the newsgroup for the benefit of new readers, but they can also be found at various FTP sites.

A couple of useful newsgroups to join at first are:

news.announce.newgroups	Provides details of newly-created groups
news.announce.newusers	The place for new users to start. Join this first!

Usenet can contain useful information, but there can also be a lot of idle chatter. Some groups are relatively 'noise' free depending on the subject matter. You can usually guess the type of things discussed in a newsgroup from its name, '`uk.jobs.offered`' being a good example.

.net Guide

World Wide Web

The World Wide Web (also known as WWW or just plain 'Web') is the brave and rather pretty new face of the Internet. Much mooted as the 'killer app' for the Internet, the WWW provides a user-friendly graphical interface to the Net. In a similar way to the 'Help' systems found in Microsoft Windows and on Apple Macintoshes, Web pages enable you to click on highlighted words which can then give you more information on that subject. It can even take you to another Web site which could be located anywhere on the globe.

A killer app (or application) is a term used to describe a 'must-have' piece of software, a package that justifies changing to the computer or system it runs on.

Web pages are written using a language called HTML or HyperText Markup Language, which looks like normal ASCII text, but contains embedded commands to do the clever stuff. The World Wide Web is a much more user-friendly way of navigating the Internet than the other, text command driven methods. By using a program called a Web Browser, you can traverse the Web with ease.

One of the most popular and feature-packed Web Browsers is called Netscape. This is currently available in versions for Windows, Apple Macs, and various UNIX-based machines. Version one is free for non-profit use, but if you use it for business you will need to pay a small licence fee. It is available for FTPing at ftp.mcom.com.

Netscape is a powerful Web Browser.

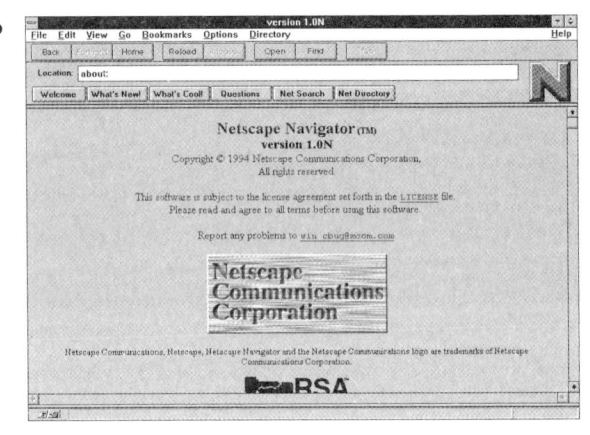

You can also use the Web to promote your business. Many companies are starting to use the Web to advertise their products or services, from monster-sized corporations to very small businesses. Most of the Internet providers offer a service in which you can rent space on their Web servers, in which you can place your own Web pages. With a little thought on design and layout, an advert on the Web can look very professional – the added advantage being that no-one can tell if you are a big company with huge, shiny offices, or a one-man band working from a spare room. The Web provides a level playing-field for doing business.

The World Wide Web is truly the future of the Internet. By giving the Internet a friendly and easy-to-use face, it will help attract more businesses and people.

Telnet

It is worth mentioning the Telnet tool briefly, as you may need to access the other features of the Net. Telnet isn't a search tool or information resource. It is a way of connecting to another machine on the Internet, and using it as if it were your own. As with all other Internet tools, you can't just connect to any old machine on the Net, it has to be set up for Telnet access. What happens once you are connected to the remote machine depends on the type of service you have connected to. In most cases you will need to log-in and details of how to do this may be displayed after you have connected to it. A useful Telnet site, especially if you are unable to access the full graphical splendour of the Web is: `telnet.w3.org`. This is a text-based Web Browsing system. Details of how to use it are displayed when you connect.

Searching for information

With such a mind-numbing amount of information accessible on the Net, you need a way to easily locate the things that interest you without running up heart attack-inducing phone bills. Luckily there are several tools that can help you search for and locate the information you want.

Web Searching

The World Wide Web has various sites that are dedicated to searching. As well as Web-specific searching, you can also access other search tools – such as Gopher, Archie and WAIS – from the comfort of the Web. With these sites, you can search for any information you might need in a much easier and more intuitive way. They are invaluable when you are after something specific, and can save you a lot of time (and money) trawling through the Web. Some of these sites are listed in the Teleworkers Directory at the back of the book.

Gopher this, Gopher that

Gopher is a tool that does just that: it 'goes for' things. More accurately it is a useful tool for locating resources on the Net. With it, you can search for on-line documents and files from gopher-connected sites all over the globe. Once it has found a file you want, it can go and retrieve it for you. You could think of it as a sort of on-line librarian. It provides you with an easy-to-navigate menu-system, which makes finding specific information easy. If you have a direct Internet connection and use a graphical Gopher client, it's simply a matter of pointing and clicking your way through the menus.

As there are many Gopher servers, some dedicated to specific subjects, it can be hard enough to get to the right place, even before you start searching. Luckily there is another search tool – a sort of Gopher for Gophers – called Veronica. This keeps an index of all the subjects covered by all available Gopher sites. You can then search this index for the subject you are interested in, giving you a much larger information base. Most Gophers have Veronica listed as a menu item, from which you can begin searching.

Wide Area Information Servers

Wide Area Information Servers, known as WAIS, are powerful search tools for on-line documents. By using WAIS you can search the contents of electronic documents stored in large on-line databases at various sites around the globe. WAIS is a very useful searching tool, as it searches inside the documents, instead of having to rely on a filename. Once you have found a document of interest, you can tell WAIS to go and get other related documents. As it could be searching through millions of words, it can be slow. But the

The Internet

results are usually worth it – and it is certainly a lot faster than looking for it yourself!

Different types of Internet connection

Without getting into a load of technical nonsense, it is worth explaining the different ways of connecting to the Net, of which there are two basic types.

The first one is the direct Internet connection, offered by companies such as Demon and Cityscape. This type of service offers a TCP/IP connection which places your machine directly on to the Internet. This is the type of service to go for if you only intend to use the Internet exclusively, or if your Internet usage will be heavy. You also need a direct TCP/IP connection if you wish to take advantage of graphical World Wide Web browsers. An important advantage of this direct connection to the Internet, is that you can perform more than one task simultaneously. For example, you can be searching for some information via the Web, downloading a file via FTP and searching for another file using Archie all at the same time (banjo playing is optional!).

> **TCP/IP (Transmission Control Protocol/Internet Protocol) is the language of the Internet. Put simply, it is the way machines on the Net exchange information. Generally, it is not available from chemists.**

Secondly, there is the terminal-based Internet connection, offered by on-line services such as Delphi or Cix. These offer an Internet 'gateway' which you can access without the need to run TCP/IP based software. With these, you can use a basic terminal program, or the service's custom software package. This method only enables you to use one Internet command at a time and only allows text-only Web browsing. This route is only recommended if you just intend to dabble with the Internet, or wish to use the on-line service itself for file transfers and the like.

Software tools for using the Net

If you intend to access the Internet via an on-line service such as Delphi or Cix, then you need no extra software other than the basic terminal program you use to dial-in, or the service's custom software if you use that.

The Internet is awash with free or shareware software utilities for using the Internet, for most popular computers. But of course, to get these tools, you need to be already on-line. It's that old chicken and egg scenario.

Your Internet provider may provide all the software you need to access the Internet, or at the very least will give you details on where and how to download software to get you started. As long as you use a reasonably popular personal computer, such as an IBM PC compatible, Macintosh, Amiga or even an Atari ST you will have no problems in finding the software you need. Contact your Internet service for details.

Getting on to the Internet

You may be thinking by now that the Internet sounds like quite a useful place to be, but are wondering just how to go about getting on the thing. Luckily, you no longer have to work for the US Government or in an academic institution. There are many Internet service providers in this country offering different types or levels of service. Each have various POPs located at different parts of the country. Where there is a POP local to you, you will be able to access the service at local call rates.

> **A POP (Point Of Presence) is a dial-access point for a service. They may physically have a machine located there, or the call may be routed to the service's main computers wherever they may be in the country.**

The on-line services that offer Internet gateways, rather than a direct connection, are listed the BBS and on-line services chapter. Here are a few of the direct Internet providers in the UK (please note that all charges are exclusive of VAT).

CityScape

Their IP-GOLD service for Windows and Mac users provides easy to set up Internet software.

POPS	London, Edinburgh, Manchester, Bristol, Birmingham and Cambridge.

Pricing	IP-GOLD has a registration fee of £50 and there is an annual membership fee of £180.

Contact	**CityScape Internet Services Ltd** 59 Wycliffe Road Cambridge CB1 3JE Telephone (sales): 01223 566950 Email: sales@cityscape.co.uk

Demon Internet

Demon were the pioneers of the direct Internet connection for the public. They are currently the largest service of this kind in the UK, with over 18,000 members.

POPS	Just about everywhere (there is even one on the Isle of Wight, bless 'em). Telephone to check there is one near you.
Pricing	Standard dial-up account has a one-off registration fee of £12.50, and the monthly charge is £10 – there are no other usage charges. Other extended services are available.
Contact	**Demon Internet** 322 Regents Park Road Finchley London N3 2QQ Telephone (sales): 0181 371 1234 or 0131 552 0344 Email: internet@demon.net

The Direct Connection

The Direct Connection also have their own on-line service which provides terminal-based Internet connection similar to the system used on Cix and Delphi.

POPS   London, Bristol, Birmingham, Cambridge, Edinburgh, Warrington.

Pricing Direct TCP/IP account has a registration fee of £15 and the monthly charge is £15 – no additional usage charges. Other types of account are available.

Contact **The Direct Connection**
PO Box 931
London
SE18 3PW

Telephone (sales): 0181 317 0100
Email: helpdesk@tdc.dircon.co.uk

Chapter 4
BBSs and On-Line Services

If the Internet seems too scary or just too much for your needs, there are other ways to transfer your information over a phone line. BBS and commercial on-line services provide easy-to-use interfaces with luxuries such as on-line help systems and people falling over themselves to assist you. The on-line services (and a few large BBSs) give you the chance to try out the Internet using only your standard comms program, meaning you don't have to bother about TCP/IP and all that nonsense.

Bulletin board systems

A Bulletin Board System (BBS for short) consists of one or more computers that can be dialled-up via a modem, providing 'areas' for message-based discussion or software files. They are normally menu-based systems and are navigated using single letter commands. It is always a good idea to check the on-line help system provided, as each BBS is different.

When you first log-on to a BBS you will be asked for your personal details and an account in your name will be created for you. Quite often your access will be limited until your account is verified (some SysOps will ring you back to check you are who you say you are). You will also need to choose a password, so think of one before you dial-up!

BBSs are run by people called SysOps, who are quite often doing it out of the kindness of their hearts. Rather than being a misspelt mythical Greek monster, this is a shortened form of System Operator. There are many privately-operated BBSs scattered all around the UK. These vary from a single machine running in somebody's bedroom, to large,

BBSs and On-Line Services

commercially-run ventures. As a rule, they don't generally have any Internet access, although a couple of the larger ones have features such as Internet email gateways.

Most BBSs cost nothing to call; a few BBSs ask you to pay a modest annual or monthly fee, especially those with extra facilities like Internet email. There are a few BBSs with premium rate call numbers (0898 type numbers). As these are charged at 39p per minute (cheap rate), it will take no time at all to run up a scary phone bill. These services are best avoided!

A lot of BBSs are connected by a network called Fidonet. This enables BBSs to pass messages amongst each other, resulting in an electronic mail system called Fidonet Mail. As these BBSs only dial-up and swap messages once a day, it is a very slow mail method compared to the Internet.

You can find advertisements for various BBSs in the computer press. Once you are on-line, it is quite simple to find details of others. Public BBSs are not a very viable tool for the teleworker. They can certainly be useful for their discussion areas and downloadable software, but not very practical for business use. They are not particularly secure by their very nature, being publicly open. Also, as most of them are run as hobbies, they are prone to unexpected temporary or permanent closure at any time.

You are most likely to use a BBS if the company you are working for operates one. This would enable you to dial-up at any time and send your files or messages directly to the company's computer. This offers a relatively cheap method of sending your work files, as you only have to pay the normal telephone charges. However, you would not have access to any of the many on-line delights that are to be had in commercial on-line services or on the Internet. It would merely be an electronic post office, but if that is all you require it is a cost-effective method.

Sitting somewhere between the Internet and BBSs are the commercial on-line services.

On-line services

There are a number of on-line services available in the UK, each offering different facilities. The biggest ones, which are the ones we will be looking at, are Cix (Compulink Information eXchange), Delphi Internet and CompuServe. Generally, these are hybrid services which operate in a similar way to a BBS, but also have varying types of Internet access. They also boast a wide range of additional features, such as large discussion areas, electronic databases and even on-line shopping. All offer the basic facilities such as electronic mail and the ability to transport your files.

These services differ from most of the direct Internet providers, as they charge depending on the amount of time you are connected to them. They do, however, provide a lot of customer help and support, both from the staff and the on-line 'communities'. Each service has a large number of message-based discussion areas, covering a vast range of subjects. In these, you can find all manner of useful information, by 'chatting' to the other users on the system. An initial message, called a 'root' message, is posted and others can post replies or 'comments' to that or subsequent messages. An electronic conversation of this kind, which flows from a single message, is called a 'thread'. You can

BBSs and On-Line Services

join the public areas by issuing the appropriate 'join area' command, but some are closed and you can only join by invitation. In that case, you would need to email the operator or 'moderator' of that area to ask to be let in.

As well as being able to access all the software available on the Internet via the FTP tool, there are a large collection of useful software programs and files to be found on the services themselves. These are contained within the message areas, and therefore are grouped into the appropriate subject types. This makes finding things very easy.

You can also create your own personal message areas. This is easiest with Cix where there are three types of conference: open (open to anybody); closed (it is in the list of conferences, but you have to ask to be let in); and closed confidential (you have to be granted access by the moderator and it is also 'hidden' from the main list of conferences). You can use your conference to swap messages with your clients or employers and also use it to send and receive files.

These on-line services also have custom-written software available, either free or for a small charge. These can offer a graphical front-end to the service, which lets you navigate the service via point and click (such as WinCIM, the Windows CompuServe Information Manager), rather than having to type nasty text commands.

Also available are a selection of programs called 'off-line readers' (OLRs). These enable you to log-on, fetch your unread messages from the conferences you are joined to and collect any waiting email – and download them in a

Chapter 4

Ameol, the official OLR for CIX.

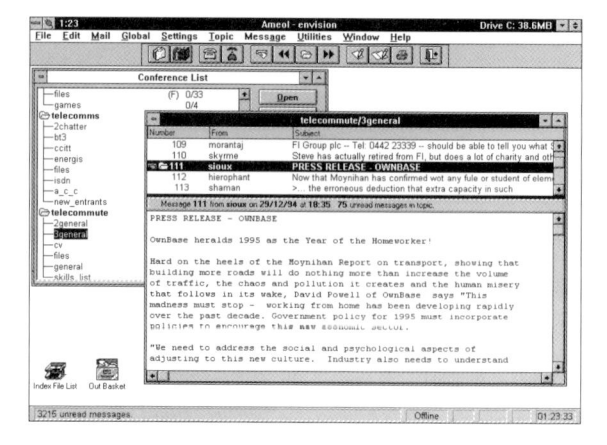

big lump. You can then use the OLR to read and reply to your messages at your leisure. When you have finished composing your replies you can upload them in the same way. These short connections are called 'blinks' which refers to their relative speed. This saves greatly on the time you are connected, thus saving you phone and on-line charges.

Here are the details for each of the on-line services covered. Please note that the prices mentioned are exclusive of VAT.

Cix

Compulink Information eXchange is the largest conferencing system based solely in the UK. It currently has a membership in excess of 15,000 and boasts over 2,500 message areas which are called conferences. Just about every subject you can think of has a conference, including one for teleworkers! Internet facilities are very good; just about everything is covered including a text-based Web browser. There are no additional charges for using the Internet gateway, just the normal on-line charges. At the

.net Guide

BBSs and On-Line Services

time of writing, Cix had just announced plans to provide a full direct Internet service. No details on price or facilities were available.

Pricing There is a £25 registration fee. On-line charges are £3.60 per hour peak rate (Monday–Friday, 8.00am–5.00pm) and £2.40 at all other times subject to a monthly minimum of £6.25.

POPS Surbiton (er, that's it).

Contact **Compulink Information Exchange**
The Sanctuary
Oakhill Grove
Surbiton
Surrey
KT6 6DU

Telephone (sales): 0181 390 8446
Email: cixadmin@cix.compulink.co.uk

CompuServe

With 2.2 million members world-wide (60,000 UK members), CompuServe is probably the biggest commercial on-line service. It offers a huge amount of message areas, called forums, and many software publishers and hardware manufacturers have their official support areas on these. There are many additional services available, from on-line databases to travel information, but most are charged as extras. CompuServe is far from being the cheapest service, but there is a wealth of information there if your wallet can handle it. Internet facilities until recently have been very limited, but plans to expand the service are under way. At present, the few Internet-based parts of the system, such as Usenet, FTP and Internet email, are subject to extra charges.

Pricing   There are a series of pricing structures for the various features on the system. The standard pricing plan costs $9.95 per month which covers unlimited connect time to Basic Services. Extended Services are charged at the rate of $4.80 per hour. All charges are made in US dollars and there are other pricing plans available. Registration is free, and navigation software is available for $25 which includes a $25 usage credit for Extended Services.

POPS   Most major city areas covered.

Contact   **CompuServe Information Service (UK)**
1 Redcliff Street
PO Box 676
Bristol
BS99 1YN

Telephone (sales): 0800 289458

Delphi Internet

Delphi Internet started life in the US, but opened a UK arm in 1994. It currently has in excess of 100,000 members world-wide. There are separate UK and US sections, but you can access one from the other with ease. It has a wide range of message forums covering many topics. Its sister-companies – Twentieth Century Fox, The Times and Fox Television – have sections on-line. There are a full range of Internet facilities available through their Internet SIG (Special Interest Group). All commands are accessed through an easy to use menu system and there is comprehensive on-line help. There are no additional charges for using the Internet facilities.

Pricing   Charges are time-based, and there are two pricing plans to choose from. The 10/4 plan costs £10 per month which includes the first four hours' use each month – after that, on-line time is charged at the rate of £4 per hour. The second plan, called 20/20, costs £20 per month. This gives you twenty hours' use, after which you will be charged at the additional rate of £1.80 per hour. Delphi currently run an introductory offer to the system which gives you five hours' free use to look around before you decide to join.

Chapter 4

The Delphi Internet SIG.

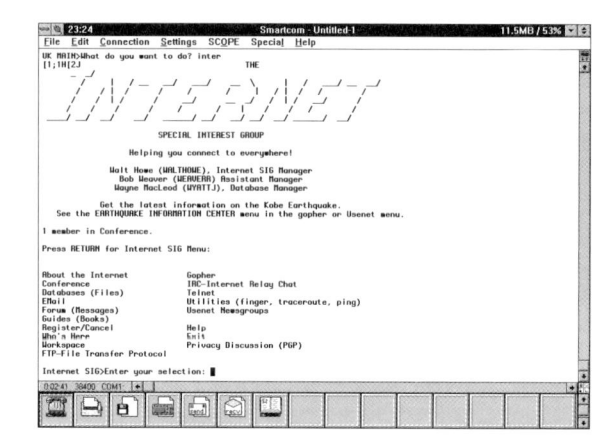

POPS — Main access point is in London, but is local-call accessible for much of the country through GNS Dialplus (which is surcharged).

Contact — **Delphi Internet UK**
The Elephant House
Hawley Crescent
London
NW1 8NP

Telephone (sales): 0171 757 7080
Email: uk@delphi.com

Chapter 5
Real World Considerations

There is a bit more to teleworking than plugging a modem into a computer and just banging out your work, sadly. Working from home is radically different from your average 9-to-5 office regime. The lack of fixed working hours and a slobbering dictator (or boss) watching your every move may at first seem very nice indeed, but this may present big potential problems for the budding home worker. Self-organisation requires effort (huge amounts for some), as does motivation and discipline.

Many teleworkers will also be running their own business, which can be known to open up a venerable jumbo-sized can of multi-segmented slimy things. This chapter looks at a few of the practicalities of teleworking from home, whether you will be self-employed or working for someone else.

Being legal and decent

No, not the type of work you do, although I'm sure that it is. There are a few legalities to be aware of when you work from home, depending on the type of work you do. Your main worry is likely to be whether you can legally use your home as a work place.

The likeliest candidate for real problems are planning regulations. Much of the red tape involved has been cut away over recent years and many of the regulations look favourably on the homeworker. The regulations are broadly divided into two parts: planning permission and building regulations.

Real World Considerations

> **WHAT DOES IT MEAN?**
>
> **A detailed series of regulations exist to protect the environment of our countryside, towns and cities. Any planned alterations to your property must comply with these regulations. If you build or alter your home without planning permission, you can be forced to reverse the change by the local authority.**

Planning permission is required for a wide range of things. In addition to building alterations, special types of planning approval are required when things such as a listed building, protected trees or a conservation site are involved.

It doesn't only relate to building alterations, such as building an extension to your house for an office. You may need planning permission if one or more of the following apply to you:

- You employ more than one person
- The major part of the house is used for business
- If your business involves noise, fumes or anti-social hours
- You have customers calling at your home on a regular basis
- You have regular deliveries from suppliers
- You need to park a trade vehicle on your premises

Planning permission is one big grey area and if you are in any doubt, you should contact your local authority for advice. It is far better to get the necessary approvals beforehand if they are needed. If you are caught without the approval you need, the local authority can close your business down.

You are only likely to face building regulations if you intend to alter the structure of your home, or add an extension to it. If, for example, you were to build an extension to house your home office, you would first need to apply for planning permission. Once that is granted, then the extension would be subject to the building regulations.

WHAT DOES IT MEAN

Building regulations are detailed rules drawn up to ensure that a new building or an alteration to an existing property is safe. Building inspectors visit the site to check that the regulations are being adhered to. Building regulations are separate from planning permission, and just because you are granted one does not mean you will necessarily be granted the other!

In general, most homeworkers will have little or no problems with planning authorities. However, other problems may arise from using your home for work.

You will need to contact your mortgage company if your home is mortgaged and you intend to use all or part of your property for business purposes. It is almost certain that if you are only using one existing room for work that they will have no objections. You may have problems if you intend to physically alter your house as it may adversely affect the value of your home. They would also be likely to have concerns if you were using more than one room for work. In such a case, as the mortgage was originally intended as a residential loan, they might then consider that it has now transformed into a commercial loan – which could then

Real World Considerations

attract a higher rate of interest. Mortgages vary from company to company, but you should inform your lender of your intentions as soon as you can.

If you don't have a mortgage, but are a tenant, you will need to check the terms of your lease to make sure there are no clauses which would prohibit you from working at home. Even if there are no such clauses, it is still a good idea to contact your landlord to inform them. As you will be teleworking, your business is likely to be paper-based, which shouldn't upset anyone. You aren't likely to damage the property with a computer and a modem!

A lot of houses, and most residential flats, contain conditions in their deeds which limit the sort of business activities you can carry out there. Some deeds specify a total ban on any sort of business being operated from the property, although most only have limits on things such as the selling of alcohol or the running of a glue factory. Even if the deeds do have a seemingly total ban on business activities, you may still be okay as it generally doesn't apply to 'learned professions' – but of course, it depends on the type of work you intend to do.

If the deeds says that you cannot engage in an 'obnoxious' or 'objectionable' business then you should also have no problems (assuming you aren't). As the deeds were drawn up when the property was new, a lot of them are quite old and therefore have restrictions which seem out of place today. Some deeds specify that you cannot run a circus from the garden, for example. On the whole, you would be very unlucky to come across any real problems with deed restrictions, but check them all the same. If you did have any such restrictions, you would be able to apply to the court to have such clauses (or covenants as those in the know call them) removed. As always, if you are in any doubt, contact a solicitor.

Needless to say, the above is only meant as an brief overview of some of the things to be aware of. If you are in any doubts about your legal position in such matters, you should seek advice from a professional adviser – such as a solicitor, an accountant or by going to the Citizen's Advice Bureau.

An excellent place for general advice is your local Citizen's Advice Bureau. They provide good professional help about a wide variety of matters for free. Check in your Yellow Pages, or at your local library, for details.

Be assured you're insured

Be warned – working from home may invalidate your current home contents insurance policy. Before you start homeworking, you should contact your insurance company and ask them if you would still be covered. In many cases, you may just have to pay a small premium (if anything) – as long as you do not intend to have customers visiting your home. In fact it is possible that you may even be able to get a reduction in the cost of your insurance premium, as some companies offer a discount if the house is occupied during the day.

Insurance schemes vary a fair amount, so you should always check the details of the one you have. Many policies have a single item limit, for example £1000 – and your computer

Real World Considerations

may well cost more than that to replace. So you must ensure the policy covers all of your business equipment. It is possible to insure your data as well, so you can claim for its value if your computer and hard drive are stolen, but these are specialist policies which may carry a high premium. If your insurance company is unable or unwilling to adapt your existing policy, shop around for another. It is essential that your equipment is properly insured because, in the event of any loss, your business will fold if you can't afford to replace the items from your own pocket.

Depending on your type of business, it may be wise to take out professional indemnity insurance. This would give you some protection should any advice you give to your clients lead to legal or financial problems for them. The cost for this type of insurance depends on the type of your business and the amount of cover you need. If a client suffers through your actions, they could sue – so if you are in a position where this can happen, you should seriously consider this type of cover.

If you work for yourself you are obviously reliant on your own efforts to bring in the cash. But what happens if you fall ill, or have an accident? Say for some reason you couldn't work for a week or two – could you survive with no income? Yes, that does sound like something an insurance agent would ask you, and indeed it is something you should plan for. There are various insurance schemes for the self-employed that provide you with an income in the event you are unable to work. The cost of such insurance would depend on the amount of income you need to receive each month, but it is a relatively small expenditure for the protection it gives you.

With the population growing older and the welfare state in some jeopardy, you may wish to consider contributing to a personal pension plan. If your income is somewhat erratic, go for a plan which allows for a high degree of flexibility. Such a plan should allow you to vary the amount of your contributions or even temporarily suspend payment of them if money is tight. Pension contributions are also tax deductible up to a certain level. An accountant or financial adviser should be able to advise you on what is best for you.

The taxman cometh

Chances are, if you are going to be a teleworker, you will also be self-employed. You should notify the Inland Revenue that you intend to become self-employed before you start, if they are not already aware of it.

Being self-employed, you have to pay the standard Income Tax on your annual profits. Your profits being, of course, all the money earnt by the business after legitimate business expenses. The profit is not the money left over after you have taken out your living expenses!

You are entitled to claim for certain purchases for your business – as long as they are solely for your business. If you have a car you will not be able to claim all expenses for it unless it is a commercial vehicle. Indeed, as a teleworker, you are unlikely to claim much, if anything, for transport costs. You cannot claim for things that are clearly not business-related. Buying a new hi-fi and trying to claim for it is not a clever idea (unless, of course, you are in the music business and can show it is used for your work). The tax man isn't daft. Larger items, such as computers, are called

Real World Considerations

capital allowances and are claimed against your tax over a period of several years.

Things you can claim for include: heating and electricity of your office, business telephone, business insurance, stationery, interest on business loans, and subscriptions to trade journals or assocations.

When you become self-employed you are responsible for paying your own National Insurance Contributions. There are two types applicable to self-employed people, called Class 2 and Class 4 Contributions. Class 2 payments are a weekly, fixed amount which can be paid via direct debit. The Class 4 payments are related to your profits and are paid at the same time as your Income Tax. These National Insurance Contributions do not give you the same benefits as those paid by an employee. You cannot claim Unemployment Benefit, for instance.

If your business turns over a certain level of money, you may have to become VAT (Value Added Tax) registered. Being registered allows you to deduct the VAT from supplies and services the business pays for. You would also have to collect VAT on behalf of the Government, which means your prices would have to include the VAT rate (which is currently 17.5%).

VAT returns have to be submitted every three months, which does entail more paperwork, so employing an accountant is likely to be essential. Some businesses that have a relatively low turnover and have been VAT registered for more than a year can apply for annual VAT accounting.

Many people get into all sorts of trouble with their tax because their paperwork is in a muddle or is badly filed. Just throwing receipts into a shoebox is not good enough. It may be worthwhile employing a part-time book-keeper to keep your records in order, which would be cheaper than getting an accountant to sort out your mess. You may also wish to consider using a software-based accounts package such as Quicken (available for MS-DOS and Windows) which would help you keep track of your financial transactions.

Although it is quite feasible for you to handle your own tax returns, you would probably be better off using the services of an accountant. They can offer advice specific to your requirements and shield you from the nasty tax man. Their fees are also tax deductible. If you are in doubt about your tax position, you should contact your local tax office for clarification.

Constructing your home office

The patronising git, I hear you say. He's going to tell me how to arrange my computer room now. Like I don't know how to put a computer on a desk. The cheek of it, rant, rave, etc. Well, yes, I am going to outline some tips for laying out your home office space, and the things you may need – there may just be some things you haven't considered!

Obviously it is possible to work from home without having a room dedicated as an office – but, quite frankly, if you did you would be a serious contender for the title of 'Slobbering Teleworking Loon Of The Year' award. Believe me, if you try

Real World Considerations

working without a room or an area set aside specifically for your business, you would probably soon regret it.

One of the most important reasons for having a room set aside for your work is to cut out any unnecessary distractions. Having a room dedicated as an office makes it easier to isolate yourself from your family or children, so you can concentrate on your work. Even if you live on your own, there are many things that can tempt you away from work. Seemingly minor distractions such as watching the morning news on the television are likely to interrupt your work-flow. Ten minutes watching the news can oh-so-easily turn into a couple of hours watching daytime drivel TV. Although it may not be remotely interesting, daytime television has a special ability to hook and transfix the viewer. They suck your working hours from you like some kind of media-vampire thing. And you really don't want that to happen, trust me.

Another good reason for having a separate room for work is that it would be simpler to claim related office expenses, such as heating and electricity. If you have 6 rooms in your house, for example, you would be able to claim for at least a sixth of the appropriate household expenses. The room has to be exclusively for your business for you to do so though. You may be able to claim a higher percentage of your electricity bill if you could show you were using a larger amount for your business. Handy if you have a particle accelerator in your office, which gobbles up electricity like nobody's business.

Design the room with only one thing in mind – your work. Do not be tempted to put a television in your office, even for occasional viewing during breaks. You will end up being transfixed by the daytime television vampire and one of the reasons for having a separate room was to escape its clutches. It will eat into your working hours, costing you time and money. Your time is valuable – just because you happen to work from home rather than an office does not make it less so. Time lost during normal working hours will eventually have to be made up from your normal leisure time. Be ruthless with yourself on this – you must focus on your work.

If you are going to be spending many hours a day at a desk, it is sensible to invest in a decent chair. It is not advisable to make do with a chair from the dining room or suchlike. Many people are guilty of thinking the type of chair is not that important – not so, it is a vital part of your office equipment. Unless you want to end up looking like something from Notre Dame, get a proper desk chair with sufficient support for your back. They may be expensive compared to cheaper, normal chairs, but it is a small price to pay for saving your back and posture. Besides, office equipment is a perfectly valid business expense and thus you can claim the cost of it against your Income Tax bill.

When it comes to choosing a desk, make sure you get one large enough to support your computer and any other dangly bits. Allow for keyboard space, room for the mouse and any other peripherals you may have (such as a modem!). Don't forget basic things like measuring the desk to make sure it will fit in your room comfortably (and you can get it through the door!). It's also a good idea to get a desk that has specially provided slots or holes for your computer cables. It makes for a tidy desk if you can feed modem or keyboard cables through a nice neat slot.

You will need to consider the type and position of the drawers the desk has as well. Choose a desk that has decent-sized drawers for any frequently needed things, such as stationary, printer paper, disks etc. Bear in mind your favoured side; left-handed people for example should ensure the drawers are positioned correctly for them. If you have a small room, the location of the drawers may be important. It isn't very funny to buy a desk only to find that you can't open the drawers because something is in the way. Also check that you have enough leg room for when you are sat at it. People of especially large dimensions (upwards, outwards, or both) need to be particularly careful about this. Don't just buy a desk because it looks nice – test drive it!

If you have the room, a second desk or an additional table can be a good idea. The main desk could be used for your computer, which would be your main work area. The extra desk could be used to support a printer or a telephone, keeping your main desk as clear as possible. You are likely to clutter your main working area with extra bits of paper as you work anyway, so it is best to start with it as clear as you can. A second desk would also be useful if you have to refer to books or papers often, so you could leave them on there and consult them quickly and easily.

If you deal with a lot of paper, some kind of filing cabinet is essential. It is far easier to find the invoice or letter you are looking for if it is indexed in a filing cabinet rather than stuffed in some old shoebox. It is also sensible to get a disk box for your computer disks as well. Much nicer and neater than piling them on the desk or floor – and it is easier to locate the disk you need as well.

Some kind of fire-resistant safe or box is a good idea for your important papers or disks. The data on a computer's hard drive is quite often more valuable than the computer equipment itself, but is rarely insured. When you make your regular backups, you could place them in a fire-proof container. If the worst did happen, at least you have a chance of retrieval. Having said that, it is far better to store your backups 'off-site' (a different building), if you value your data.

Shelving. Lovely shelving. If, like me, you have a mountain of books and papers, then good shelving is a must. Shelving takes all the potential clutter from your desk area and attaches it to the wall out of harm's way. Ensure you have sufficient shelf space for all your current bits and pieces, plus extra depending on how much your book, software or magazine collections grow. Can't get enough of it. Lovely.

A thing not often considered is the lighting of the room. You are likely to be spending many hours working in your room, so lighting conditions are important for the sake of your eyes. You also need to position your computer monitor so that it doesn't reflect any glare from a window or from another light source. Bad lighting will cause you eye-strain which could well lead to headaches. It could also give you a nasty squint which will make children in the street scream and run away from you.

Another vital piece of office equipment for the budding teleworker is, unsurprisingly a computer.

Choosing a computer

Pretty much any modern personal computer will do for getting on-line – provided it has a RS-232 type serial port or another means of connecting it to a modem, and it has the communications software you need available for it. It is very much down to personal taste and how much you are willing to spend. Some people can get quite fanatical about their particular type of computer, almost to the point of telling you that it can cure all known diseases. But sensible computers users will tell you that different computer systems have different strengths and weaknesses, as with any other type of equipment.

By far the most popular and thus most widely supported type of computer is the IBM PC compatible. It has undoubtedly the most choice in terms of software and add-on hardware. If you are unsure about which computer to buy, the PC is generally a safe bet. But there are hundreds of PC manufacturers, and it can be hard to tell their systems apart. If you are thinking of getting such a system, it is best to read one or two of the many PC-based magazines beforehand, as well as chatting to any people you know who use them.

> **MAKE A NOTE!** **If you are going to be using a PC compatible machine and will be running Windows, make sure it has something called a 16550 UART chip inside it. This is an enhanced serial port chip, and is essential for fast, reliable comms under Windows.**

Some computers are better suited to particular types of work and this should be taken into account when buying a computer. For example, Apple Macs are generally considered to be better tools for digital audio and video work than IBM PCs, as well as being very widely used in the professional and desktop publishing markets. Your employer or clients may insist on you using a particular software package which is only available on a specific computer system. They may even insist that you use a particular sort of system anyway, in which case you don't have any choice. At the very least, the files that you send to them must be usable on their computers, so this needs to be considered when choosing your machine.

If you intend using a computer for your work, you will need a hard disk drive. Hard drive prices have fallen sharply recently, and quite largish drives can be had for a relatively lost cost per megabyte. Make sure you get a big enough drive for your needs. It is far better to spend a few extra pounds for an extra 50 or 100Mb than to run out of space and have to get a new drive. If you are running Windows or a similar graphical user interface operating system, it is a good idea to get a drive in the 400-500Mb range. This may seem like an awful lot of space, but some software packages need over 20Mb just for the program files! Also, if you start downloading some of the software that is on the Net, it will fill up in no time – believe me!

Some computer systems come with a monitor screen, some don't – you need to check this. Some of the smaller home computers give you the option of connecting to a television instead of using a dedicated monitor. But for any serious amount of computer work, this is not recommended. Your eyes will suffer if they are forced to squint at the relatively low resolution of a television screen. Besides, you might be

Real World Considerations 89

tempted to switch channels to watch the Sooty show instead of working – and we can't have that.

The type of computer you need is something only you can decide. Talk to as many people you know who already have computers as well as dealers before deciding. You will be investing several hundreds or even thousands of pounds, so take your time and make sure that the system can do everything you need, or will need it to do. The past is littered with people having bought a computer purely because 'a mate has got one' only to find it completely inadequate for their needs.

If you plan to telework from home, you'll can't really do without...

A telephone line

You know what a phone line is. Of course you do. But you may have choices you didn't realise you had when it comes to the phone service you use. You are not necessarily tied to using British Telecom any more. Depending on where you live, you may be able to use a cheaper telephone service for your local or long-distance calls.

British Telecom and others offer various discount schemes for frequent telephone users. One such scheme offers an automatic 5% discount for calls made to five user-nominated numbers. For example, you could nominate one or more of your on-line services telephone numbers and you would then save 5% on your call

#4 Teleworking .net

charges whilst on-line. Contact your phone service to see what current discount options they offer.

Another option, depending on where you live, is to use the phone services offered by some of the various cable companies. Several of these offer such goodies as free local calls after a certain time of the day, which would be rather lovely if your Internet Provider or on-line service also subscribed to them. Some of these companies also offer special services for business users, and it is worth ringing up the relevant sales line to inquire about their current services.

If you use the same phone line for home and business, you need to ensure that none of your family members try to use the phone whilst you are. It would be very embarrassing and would look quite unprofessional if someone was to pick-up and dial from another extension whilst you were in the middle of a call to a client.

You may wish to consider using a second, dedicated phone for your teleworking. As well as leaving a free line for you to receive voice calls whilst on-line, it makes things easier for when claiming it as a business expense. If you have a fax modem, you could also leave it in answer mode to receive any incoming faxes. Plus of course, it looks good on your business letterhead!

ISDN

The Integrated Services Digital Network (ISDN), mentioned earlier, offers a new, digital-based telephone service.

Real World Considerations

Although it is handled digitally by the exchange, it still uses the old copper wires in your home – so it is something of a compromise.

There are two types of service currently available called ISDN-2 and ISDN-30. ISDN-2 offers two separate data channels which can be used together or individually, whereas ISDN-30 gives you 30 (!). So unless you are part of a very large business, you are more likely to use ISDN-2. Each line or channel is capable of transmitting up to 64K per second – quite a bit faster than even V.34! You can also combine both channels to get 128K per second – and that is before any data compression.

You may be thinking that as ISDN is digital, you won't need a modem. Well, you would be right – sort of. Instead of a modem, you need to use something called a terminal adapter to interface with your computer. Some of these have analogue ports which will allow you to connect your existing telephone and equipment to ISDN. But these are currently very expensive and there are some problems with the standards.

At the current time, ISDN costs more to install than a regular phone line, and has a higher quarterly rental – but the call charges are the same as normal. If you use both channels though, you will be charged at twice the rate. Although ISDN has been available for a while now, it is far from straightforward. If you think you need the power of ISDN, I strongly urge you to seek some expert advice.

Chapter 6
Where Do I Go From Here?

It is a good idea to stop and think what it means to be a teleworker. Some people have misconceptions about what teleworking can actually do for them. But it should be stressed, in huge pink neon lights, that teleworking is not a type of job – it is a way of working. A question often asked by potential teleworkers is 'How can I get a teleworking job?' This is akin to asking 'How can I get a commuting job?' – which is plainly a daft question. This is not the way to look at teleworking.

The very first thing you should do is think long and hard about whether the work that you currently do, or aim to do, will benefit from the telecommunications advantages offered by using a computer and modem. You then need to consider the sort of on-line service which best suits your needs. If you are interested in having access to a huge amount of information and think you will be spending a fair amount of time on-line – then a direct Internet service would best fulfil your requirements. But setting up a direct Internet connection can be tricky, even for those used to computers. Commercial on-line services such as Cix and Delphi are better suited to beginners or for occasional jaunts on to the Internet.

It would be a good idea to contact one of the various teleworking associations, especially if there is one local to you and chat to them about your plans. They have been down this path themselves and may be able to point out things you might not have considered. If you are serious about wanting to telework, there is no shortage of people who can help you set up and adjust to this working method.

If you don't yet have a computer, then of course you need to get one before going any further. A computer is a major purchase for a business and it will probably have to last for a good few years, so choose very carefully. Don't take one person's advice on which to buy – get as many opinions as you can. Make sure you ask lots of questions – make a nuisance of yourself if you have to – but be certain you are investing in the right machine for you.

If you decide to take that step into the future, and join the ever-growing number of home-workers who put the 'tele' in front of 'commute' – then I wish you every success. The transition may not be a painless one, but it will be an exciting one. Oh, and I'll be expecting some email from you, once you get on-line.

Chapter 7
A Teleworkers Directory

Real world resource guide

Here is a useful directory for teleworkers, which lists resources both on-line and in the real world. This is a selection of some of the groups, associations and journals that are available for helping the teleworker.

Home Run

This is a monthly publication aimed at the home office worker. Launched in October 1992, it is the UK's leading journal for those who work from home. It is packed full of useful information and is well worth the subscription.

Membership fee   £48 per annum for individuals
£72 per annum for corporates
Comes with a two-issue money-back guarantee

Contact   **Active Information**
79 Black Lion Lane
London
W6 9BG

Telephone/Fax: 0181 846 9244
Email: 100117.27@compuserve.com

National Association of Teleworkers

The NAT provides a range of services, including a teleworking code of practice. Members receive a quarterly newsletter and copies of the European Journal of Teleworking.

A Teleworkers Directory

Membership fee £46.94 per annum

Contact **National Association of Teleworkers**
The Island House
Midsomer Norton
Bath
BA3 2HL

Telephone: 0404 47467
Email: 100063.462@compuserve.com

OwnBase

This is a network of people working from home, who exchange information and provide benefits such as pensions and training to its members. It aims to raise awareness of the requirements of home-based workers. They also publish a newsletter several times a year.

Membership fee £24.50 per annum

Contact **The Enquiries Department**
OwnBase
68 First Avenue
Bush Hill Park
Enfield
EN1 1BN
(Enclose SAE)

Telephone/Fax: 0181 363 0808
Email: sioux@cix.compulink.co.uk

Teleworking Special Interest Group

Partly funded by the DTI, this group provides a forum for the exchange of information on teleworking issues. It aims to actively promote teleworking through seminars and other media. It also runs a mailing list, which is listed in the on-line part of this directory.

Membership fee   Free

Contact   **Teleworking SIG**
211 Piccadilly
London
W1V 9LD

Telephone: 0171 917 2920

The Telecottage Association

The Telecottage Association provides practical advice and information for teleworkers whether they work alone or run telecottages. Members receive a fact file, a bi-monthly newsletter and access to a BBS.

Membership fee   £24.50 per annum

Contact   **The Telecottage Association**
WREN Telecottage
Stonleigh Park
Warwickshire
CV8 2RR

Telephone: 0800 616008
Email: Simon_Berry@midnet.com

On-line resource guide

This guide is not intended as a comprehensive directory of all things connected to teleworking or business on the Internet, or the on-line services. As new sites appear all the time, such a thing would be impossible. This is meant to give you a taste of what's out there and to give you a place to get started. Once you get on-line you will be able to use some of these sites as pointers to other, newer places of interest.

Internet Directory

For the Internet sites, I have used URLs as they are the standard way of addressing Net resources.

A URL or Uniform Resource Locator consists of two parts, which tell what type of Internet resource it is and its exact address on the Net. These two parts are separated by a '://' – the part before that is the resource descriptor, which tells us what type of address it is – the second part is the address. Examples of resource descriptors are: 'ftp', 'gopher', 'telnet' (which are self-explanatory), as well as 'http' (which refers to a World Wide Web site) and 'mailto' (which is for email and mailing lists). For example, Demon's public directory on their FTP server would be:

`ftp://ftp.demon.co.uk/pub`

Remember that it is only the address part you actually need to type in.

To subscribe to a mailing list, you need to email the address listed with a message saying '`JOIN <name of list> <your name>`'. For addresses that use 'listserv' use '`SUB`' instead of join.

Subject	**Advertising On-Line**
Description	Apollo Advertising's Web-based advertising services, based in the UK.
URL	`http://apollo.co.uk/home-uk.html`

Subject	**Archie**
Description	An easy-to-use Archie searcher, accessible from the Web. A 'forms compatible' browser is needed to use this resource.
URL	`http://web.nexor.co.uk/archie.html`

Subject	**Business on the Internet (1)**
Description	This Web site deals with the commercial use of the Internet.
URL	`http://pass.wayne.edu/business.html`

Subject	**Business on the Internet (2)**
Description	CommerceNet is a World Wide Web business centre.
URL	`http://www.commerce.net`

Subject:	**Business on the Internet (3)**
Description	World Wide Yellow Pages is a Web directory of businesses.
URL	`http://www.yellow.com`

.net Guide

A Teleworkers Directory

CommerceNet home page.

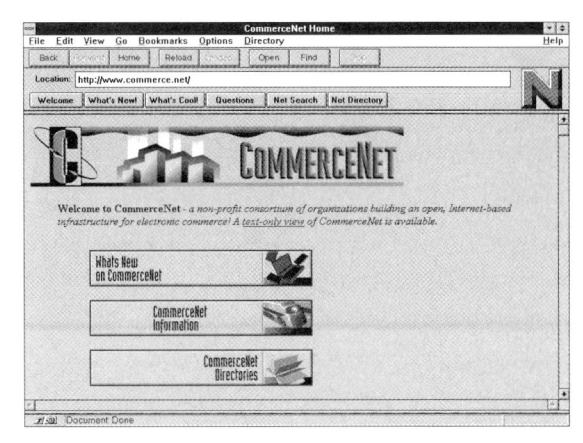

Subject	**Databases**
Description	Where to find free and commercial databases on the Net.
URL	`gopher://sunic.sunet.se`

Subject	**Demon Internet FTP**
Description	Demon's FTP site holds many useful Internet-related files.
URL	`ftp://ftp.demon.co.uk`

Subject	**Entrepreneurs**
Description	A Web site for all you entrepreneurs!
URL	`http://sashimi.wwa.com/~notime/eotw/EOTW.html`

Subject	**FTP By Email**
Description	A way to get files from FTP sites using email. Send a mail message to this address with 'help', followed by 'quit' on the next line.
URL	`mailto://ftpmail@src.doc.ic.ac.uk`

The Internet Business
Centre Web site.

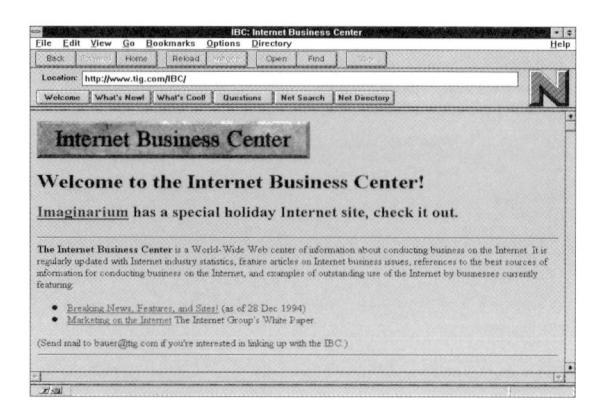

Subject	Internet Business Centre
Description	A Web site all about conducting business on the Internet.
URL	`http://www.tig.com/IBC/`

Subject	Internet Business Journal
Description	A mailing list that distributes extracts from the 'Internet Business Journal'. The name of the list is 'IBJ-L'.
URL	`mailto://listserv@poniecki.berkely.edu`

Subject	Mailing Lists (1)
Description	A mailing list that announces new mailing lists. The name of the list to subscribe to is 'new-list'.
URL	`mailto://listserv@vm1.nodak.edu`

Subject	Mailing Lists (2)
Description	Another mailing list that announces new lists, but this one is UK-based. The list name is 'new-lists'.
URL	`mailto://mailbase@mailbase.ac.uk`

A Teleworkers Directory

The Teleworkers Yellow Pages.

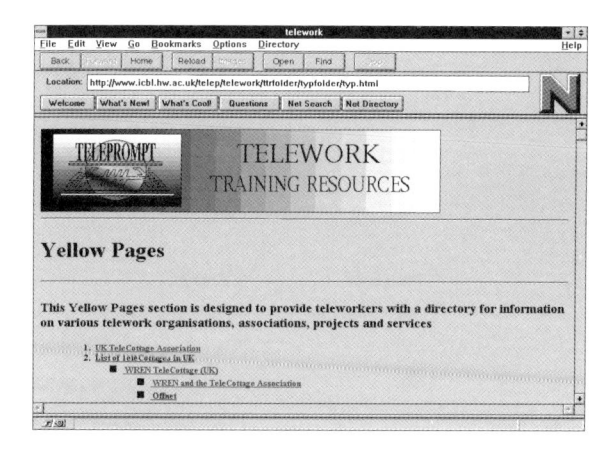

Subject	**Marketing**
Description	This Web site features electronic marketing.
URL	http://www.gems.com

Subject	**Teleworking (1)**
Description	Teleprompt teleworking training resources Web site.
URL	http://www.icbl.hw.ac.uk/telep/telework/conts.html

Subject	**Teleworking (2)**
Description	The 'Teleworkers Yellow Pages' is a useful on-line resource for teleworkers.
URL	http://www.icbl.hw.ac.uk/telep/telework/ttrfolder/typfolder/typ.html

Subject	**Teleworking (3)**
Description	Regiodesk Ireland is a help desk and information service for teleworkers supported by the Directorate XII of the EU.
URL	http://www.regiodesk.ie

#4 Teleworking .net

Subject	**Teleworking Special Interest Group**
Description	The Teleworking SIG aim is to promote teleworking through a variety of events. The list name is 'TELEWORK'
URL	`mailto://mailbase@mailbase.ac.uk`
Subject	**WAIS**
Description	A Web-accessible WAIS searching site. A very useful resource tool.
URL	`http://www.wais.com/directory-of-servers.html`
Subject	**World Wide Web Search Engine**
Description	An easy-to-use search tool for finding Web pages of interest. Requires a 'forms compatible' Web browser such as Netscape or Mosaic.
URL	`http://cuiwww.unige.ch/w3catalog`

Usenet Newsgroups

uk.jobs	The UK jobs newsgroup
uk.jobs.contract	Forum for contract workers - including advertising of contracts.
uk.jobs.offered	Various UK-based jobs adverised in here
uk.legal	Handy for if you have any legal queries

BT Phonebase

BT Phonebase allows you to use your modem for directory enquiries. You get access to up-to-date information, compared to a paper-based 'phone book that can be up to a year old. Calls to the service are charged at long distance rates and it only supports 2400 BPS connections. But the service costs nothing to join and compared to the high cost of voice-based Directory Enquiry calls, it could save you money.

Telephone: (0800) 919 199 to request details.

On-line services directory

Here are a selection of the conferences or forums that may be of interest to a teleworker. The words in brackets show how to get to that area from the main screen of the service.

CIX

- The Own Business Conference (JOIN OWN.BUSINESS) is devoted to all aspects of running your own business.

- Telecommute (JOIN TELECOMMUTE) is a conference all about teleworking, funnily enough.

- The Contractors Conference (JOIN CONTRACT) discusses issues concerning contractors, freelancers and consultants.

- OwnBase also has a closed conference on CIX for its members.

CompuServe

- Business Database Plus (GO BUSDB) offers searches of business journals and newsletters, but at a surcharge. Includes articles on teleworking.

- Entrepreneur's Small Business Forum (GO SMALLBIZ) offers help and advice for all small businesses, including teleworkers.

- Telework Europa Forum (GO TWEUROPA) is a forum devoted to European teleworkers.

- Working From Home Forum (GO WORK) is aimed squarely at the teleworker and offers very good advice (although American in content).

Delphi

- Self Employment (US CUSTOM 276) is a forum devoted to those in self-employment.

- Small UK Business (FORUM SMALL) offers discussion on all aspects of running a small business in the UK.

- The Small Business Advertising Forum (US CUSTOM 262) is a forum devoted to promoting your business.

- Work At Home (US CUSTOM 139) covers discussions on home working, including teleworking.

- Delphi also has a section devoted to various business and finance forums (BUSINESS).

Chapter 8
Reference Section

Care in the (on-line) community

CommUnity is the Computer Communicators' Association, and came into being in the final few weeks of 1992. There had been a threat to the survival of Bulletin Board Systems from the combined forces of FAST (the Federation Against Software Theft) and ELSPA (the European Leisure Software Publishers' Association).

In an effort to try and reduce software theft and piracy, which these organisations perceived was rife on BBSs, they were looking at the possibility of getting legislation to enforce the licensing of Bulletin Boards and On-Line Systems. The on-line community soon heard about these plans, helped along the way by an article Davey Winder wrote on the subject for Amiga Shopper magazine. They decided that they needed a concerted effort to ensure such legislation should not be allowed to threaten the existence of BBSs (many of which are run on small budgets, without charging their members, and who would have to close if forced to pay a hefty licence fee every year). The result of this was a meeting in London with representatives of all the main networks. A committee was elected to investigate what could be done, and how to do it. Davey Winder was part of the steering group.

It was from these seeds that CommUnity, The Computer Communicators' Association was born. Fortunately, the proposed legislation got nowhere, and following a meeting with FAST, ELSPA, an MP, and members of the on-line community, the plans were dropped. CommUnity however has continued to grow from strength to strength, and is the UK's leading organisation of and for users of on-line systems and networks. With a regular electronic journal called CommUnicator and a presence on many BBSs as well as the Internet, will surely continue so to do.

The aims of the Computer Communicators' Association are:

1) To maintain and connect a membership which shares a common concern that access to technology, information, and communication should be as freely available as possible.

2) To raise public awareness about issues and opportunities arising from ongoing rapid advances in computer-based communications media.

3) To monitor and inform the press and media of computer-based communications, responding to misinformation or prejudice with a coherent voice.

4) To develop among policy makers a better understanding of the issues underlying free and open telecommunications, and support legal and structural approaches which ease the assimilation of new technologies by society, and maintain open access to them.

5) To support litigation in the public interest to preserve, protect, and extend civil rights within the realm of computing and telecommunications technology.

6) To work with agencies and individuals who share our interest in the development of computer-based communications.

7) To extend our membership and organisation to include wider Europe, or assist there in the establishment and networking of independent groups sharing our aims.

8) To encourage and support educational activities and initiatives which increase popular understanding of the opportunities and challenges posed by developments in computing and telecommunications.

9) To encourage and support the development of new tools which ease access to computer-based telecommunications.

The CommUnity constitution also leaves us in no doubt as to what the Computer Communicators' Association isn't, stating that they:

"...shall not seek to control or enforce specific conduct in computer communications users, on-line systems or networks. Shall not enter into any relationship with any other group wherein it becomes required, encouraged or obliged to actively monitor on-line systems, networks or activities for any person. Shall not act as intermediary between complainants or informants and other groups or agencies for the purpose of passing on allegations of, information on, or evidence of activities by computer communications users, on-line services or networks."

To find out more about CommUnity you can send email to `community@arkham.demon.co.uk` or join the Usenet Newsgroup `uk.org.community`

Files relating to CommUnity are available by FTP from:

`ftp.demon.co.uk/pub/archives/community`

The Computer Communicators' Association was originally set up as a voluntary organisation, but funds are always needed to cover the basic administrative costs and to help with lobbying. So to do your bit in ensuring that your rights as an on-line user are protected, why not join CommUnity by sending a cheque for £10.00 (£5.00 if unemployed or a student) made payable to "CommUnity" to the following address:

**CommUnity
7 Primrose Road
Halton
Leeds LS15 7RS**

Enclose a short, signed letter requesting membership which must include the following details: full name, postal address, email address, and any other information you think may be useful along with your permission to store these details in the CommUnity membership database.

Smiley dictionary

It can be very difficult to express emotional content within a plain text message, and very easy to interpret a message the wrong way. A system of "smileys" (or emote-icons for any of our American friends reading this) has been developed and is now in widespread use. A smiley is a small face made of standard characters, (turn the page sideways if you still don't 'see' them), and can help convey feelings ranging from sad to mad to glad. There are also now smileys to cover much more than just these standard emotions, and as you can see from this dictionary they are not all to be taken too seriously.

Smiley	Meaning
:-||	Angry
(:-)	Bald
:-)	Basic happy
:-(	Basic sad
B-)	Batman
:-)>	Bearded
%+(	Beaten up
?-)	Black eye
:-)X	Bow tie
R-)	Broken glasses
:^)	Broken nose
|:-)	Bushy eyebrows
)	Cheshire cat
<|-)	Chinese
3:-)	Cow
:-t	Cross
X-)	Cross-eyed
:'-(	Crying
i-)	Detective (private eye)
:-e	Disappointed
:-)'	Drooling
{:V	Duck
<:-)	Dumb question
5:-)	Elvis
>:-)	Evil grin
:'''-(	Floods of tears
:-!	Foot in mouth

.net Guide

Reference Section

/:-)	French
8)	Frog
::-)	Glasses wearer (1)
8-)	Glasses wearer (2)
8:)	Gorilla
:-')	Has a cold (1)
:*)	Has a cold (2)
:-|	Hmmmph!
:-C	Jaw hits floor
.-)	Keeping an eye out
:-#	Kiss (1)
:-*	Kiss (2)
:-X	Kiss (3)
:+)	Large nose
:-D	Laughing out loud
:-}	Leering
(-:	Left-handed
:-9	Licking lips
:-}	Lipstick wearer
:-|	Monkey
:-{	Moustache (1)
:-#)	Moustache (2)
(-)	Needs haircut
:^)	Nose out-of-joint
:8)	Pig
:-?	Pipe smoker
=:-)	Punk
:-"	Pursed lips
|-]	Robocop
O:-)	Saint
:-@	Screaming
:-O	Shocked
:-V	Shouting
|-)	Sleeping

#4 Teleworking .net

:-i	Smoker (1)
:-Q	Smoker (2)
:-j	Smoker smiling
:-6	Sour taste in mouth
:-v	Speaking
:-w	Speaks with forked tongue
*-)	Stoned
:-T	Tight-lipped
:-p	Tongue-in-cheek
:-&	Tongue-tied
:-/	Undecided
:-[	Vampire (1)
:-|<	Vampire (2)
:-<	Vampire (3)
:-)=	Vampire (4)
:-))	Very happy
:-((	Very sad
:-c	Very unhappy
C|:-)	Wearing bowler hat
d:-)	Wearing cap
[:-)	Wearing headphones
:-(#)	Wears teeth braces
;-)	Winking
:-7	Wry smile
|-O	Yawning

Acronym dictionary

Because time equals money, and never more so than in the world of on-line communications, people have devised ways of saving typing time by reducing common phrases into acronyms. These are known as TLAs, or Three Letter Acronyms, although many are not truly acronyms at all and

.net Guide

Reference Section

very few actually have three letters. Oh well, such is life. There is a whole lorry-load of these TLAs around, and I dare say that I have missed some. But I hope that this dictionary will cover the ones that are in most common usage and it should go a long way to help you make sense of some seemingly senseless terms.

Acronym	Meaning
AFAICT	As Far As I Can Tell
AFAIK	As Far As I Know
AFK	Away From Keyboard
AIUI	As I Understand It
B4	Before
BAK	Back At Keyboard
BBL	Be Back Later
BCNU	Be seeing you
BRB	Be Right Back
BSF	But Seriously Folks
BST	But Seriously Though
BTDT	Been There Done That
BTSOOM	Beats The Shit Out Of Me
BTW	By The Way
BWQ	Buzz Word Quotient
CLM	Career Limiting Move
CUL	See you later
DWIM	Do What I Mean
DWISNWID	Do What I Say Not What I Do
DYJHIW	Don't You Just Hate It When...
ESAD	Eat Shit And Die
ETLA	Extended Three Letter Acronym
EOF	End Of File
F2F	Face to Face
FAQ	Frequently Asked Question

FFS	For Fucks Sake
FOAD	Fuck Off And Die
FOAF	Friend Of A Friend
FOC	Free Of Charge
FUBAR	Fucked Up Beyond All Recognition
FWIW	For What It's Worth
FYA	For Your Amusement
FYE	For Your Entertainment
FYI	For Your Information
<G>	Grin
GA	Go Ahead
GAL	Get A Life
GIGO	Garbage In Garbage Out
GR&D	Grinning Running & Ducking
HHOJ	Ha Ha, Only Joking
HHOS	Ha Ha, Only Serious
IAE	In Any Event
IANAL	I Am Not A Lawyer
IBN	I'm Buck Naked
IIRC	If I Recall Correctly
IMBO	In My Bloody Opinion
IME	In My Experience
IMHO	In My Humble Opinion
IMNSHO	In My Not So Humble Opinion
IMO	In My Opinion
IOW	In Other Words
IRL	In Real Life
ISTM	It Seems To Me
ISTR	I Seem To Recall
ITRO	In The Region Of
ITRW	In The Real World
IWBNI	It Would Be Nice If
IYSWIM	If You See What I Mean
JAM	Just A Minute

Reference Section

KISS	Keep It Simple, Stupid
L8R	Later
LOL	Laughs Out Loud
MFTL	My Favourite Toy Language
MORF	Male Or Female?
MOTAS	Member Of The Appropriate Sex
MOTOS	Member Of The Opposite Sex
MOTSS	Member Of The Same Sex
MUD	Multi User Dungeon
MUG	Multi User Game
NALOPKT	Not A Lot Of People Know That
NFWM	No Fucking Way Man!
NIFOC	Nude In Front Of Computer
NRN	No Reply Necessary
OAO	Over And Out
OBTW	Oh, By The Way
OEM	Original Equipment Manufacturer
OIC	Oh, I See
OMG	Oh My God
OTOH	On The Other Hand
OTT	Over The Top
PD	Public Domain
PITA	Pain In The Arse
POD	Piece Of Data
RFD	Request For Discussion
ROFL	Rolls On Floor Laughing
RSN	Real Soon Now
RTFAQ	Read The FAQ
RTFM	Read The Fucking Manual
RUOK	Are you OK
SITD	Still In The Dark
SMOP	Small Matter Of Programming
SNAFU	Situation Normal, All Fucked Up
SNR	Signal to Noise Ratio

SO	Significant Other
SOL	Shit Outta Luck
STFU	Shut The Fuck Up
TANSTAAFL	There Ain't No Such Thing As A Free Lunch
TCB	Trouble Came Back
TDM	Too Damn Many
TIA	Thanks In Advance
TIC	Tongue In Cheek
TLA	Three Letter Acronym
TNX	Thanks
TPTB	The Powers That Be
TTFN	Ta Ta For Now
TTYL	Talk To You Later
TVM	Thanks Very Much
UBD	User Brain Damage
VC	Virtual Community
VR	Virtual Reality
WIBNI	Would It Be Nice If
WRT	With Regard To
WTF	What The Fuck
WTH	What The Hell
WYSIWYG	What You See Is What You Get
YABA	Yet Another Bloody Acronym
YHBM	You Have Bin Mail
YHM	You Have Mail

Reference Section

Jargon busting

One of the most annoying things when reading books on any specialist subject is that the author oftens assumes a degree of technical knowledge, with regard to jargon, on the part of the reader. We don't assume, nor would we expect, that the readers of this book will be aware of every term used in this book. Therefore we have compiled what we hope you will agree is a very handy and comprehensive glossary of Internet and comms terminology. You should be able to locate any word that you are unsure of here and find its meaning.

Glossary

ACK	An acknowledgement number carried in the TCP header that tells a TCP sender the sequence number of the byte which the TCP receiver expects next.

Address	Either the address of a user of a system, as in an email address (required so the message sent can be directed to a particular person) or the address of a site on the Internet.

AFS	A set of protocols, similar to NFS, that allow for the use of files on another network machine as if they were on your local machine.

Analogue Loopback	A modem self test which tests the modem's originate or answer frequency.
Analogue Signals	Continuous but varying waveforms, an example being the voice tones transmitted over a telephone line.
ANSI	American National Standards Institute, responsible for approving standards in many areas.
Anonymous FTP	Anonymous FTP allows a user to retrieve files from another site on the Internet without having to establish a userid and password on the system.
Application	A piece of software that performs a useful function.
Arc	To create a compressed archive of a file, or group of files, using the PKARC compression program. Now very dated, but many arc'ed files are still to be found on the Internet.
Archie	A system for finding publicly available files for FTP over the Internet.

.net .net Guide

Reference Section

Archive — A file, or group of files, that have been compressed to form one smaller file. Depending on the program used to compress the archive, it will bear one of many file extensions, including .lha .zip .arc .zoo .tar

ARPA — Advanced Research Projects Agency, part of the United States Department of Defence.

ARPAnet — The experimental network upon which the Internet was based.

ARQ — Automatic Repeat Request. An error control protocol used by Miracom modems.

ASCII — American Standard Code for Information Interchange. A code supported by just about every computer manufacturer to represent letters, numbers, and special characters.

Asynchronous — A form of data transmission which allows information to be sent at irregular intervals.

Bandwidth — The difference in Hertz between the highest and lowest frequencies of a transmission channel. Usually

	used to describe the amount of traffic through a particular newsgroup or conference.
Bang Path	An old UUCP email address system.
Barf	A failure to work!
Baseband	A digital signalling technique used in Ethernet local area networks.
Baud	Unit of measurement denoting the number of transitions in modem signals per second. Each transition may carry more than one bit of information.
BBS	Bulletin Board System.
Bigot	A common character type found in Cyberspace.
Bit	A unit of measurement that represents one character of data. A bit is the smallest unit of storage in a computer.
BITNET	An IBM based academic computer network. BITNET is an acronym for "Because It's Time, NETwork"
Bits Per Second	The speed at which bits are transmitted.

Reference Section

Blinking — Using an Off Line Reader to access an online system.

Block — Data consisting of a fixed number of characters or records, moved as a single unit during transmission.

Bogus — Non functional, or not nice.

Bounce — When email is returned due to a failure to deliver.

Bridge — A device that connects two or more physical networks and forwards packets between them.

Broadband — A transmission method often used to send different kinds of signal at the same time, like voice and data for example.

Buffer — A memory area used as a temporary storage device for data during input/output operations.

Byte — A group of binary digits that are stored and operated upon as a unit.

Cable — A bunch of insulated wires with end connectors, an example being a serial cable.

Carrier	A signal of continuous frequency capable of being modulated with another information carrying signal.
CCITT	International Consultative Committee for Telegraphy and Telephony. An organisation that produces international technical standards for data communications. Has recently been replaced by the ITU-T.
Cello	A World Wide Web graphical browser program for Windows users.
Character	A binary representation of a letter, number or symbol.
CIM	The CompuServe Information Manager is the officially supported off line reader and system navigator for CompuServe.
CI$	See also "CIS". The dollar sign replaces the "S" in this slang version, due to the cost of using the service.
CIS	CompuServe, the American online information service.

Reference Section

Cix — Compulink Information eXchange. The largest conferencing system in the UK.

CIX — The Commercial Internet Exchange, an agreement amongst Internet Service Providers regarding the commercial use of the Internet. Not to be confused with the Compulink Information eXchange although it quite often is as they share the same acronym.

Cixen — People who use the Compulink Information eXchange.

Client — An application that extracts information from a server on your behalf.

CommUnity — The Computer Communicators' Association, set up to protect and further computer communications in the UK. Similar in aims to the EFF, but with a UK perspective.

COM — A code in MS-DOS that refers to a serial port.

Compress — A UNIX archiving program that "compresses" the size of a file.

Conference	A message area, or forum, on a conferencing system like Cix. Each conference covers a defined subject matter, and is further subdivided into topics of more specific subject matter. For example, there may be a Sooty conference which has topics of Sooty, Sweep, and Sue.

Connect Time	The length of time you spend on-line to the Internet.

Cookie	A random quote, generated by software. Found on many online systems.

CoSy	CoSy is the operating system that online services like Cix and BIX are based upon. It is a shortening of the words "Conferencing System".

CPS	Characters Per Second. A measurement of data output speed.

Crash	A sudden and total system failure.

CRC	Cyclic Redundancy Checking. A type of error detection.

CREN	The Corporation for Research and Educational Networking, which

Reference Section

	was formed by a merger of BITNET and CSNET.
Cross post	To post the same message to more than one conference, message area, newsgroup.
CTS	Clear To Send, an RS-232C signal that basically means that everything is Ok for transmission of data.
Cyberpunk	A person who "lives" in the future culture of Cyberspace, Virtual Reality etc. As epitomised by the works of Bruce Sterling.
Cyberspace	A term coined by William Gibson in his novel "Neuromancer" used to describe the collective "World" of networked computers. Now commonly used to refer to the world that exists within computer networks, accessed by comms technology. My favourite definition is simply "the electric domain".
Daemon	A program which sits on a system waiting to automatically perform a specific function. Daemon is an acronym for "Disk and Execution MONitor".
DARPA	The Defence Advanced Research Projects Agency, responsible for the

development of ARPANET which was the basis of what was to develop into the Internet.

DASD — Direct Access Storage Device.

Data Compression — The compression of information to decrease transferred file size. MNP5 and V.42bis are the best known types.

Datagram — The primary unit of information transferred over the Internet using the Internet Protocol.

DCE — Data Communications Equipment.

Decryption — Decoding encrypted data to its original form.

Dial-Up — To connect to another computer by calling it over the telephone network.

DIP Switch — Dual Interface Poll switch which enables the user to set various parameters of a circuit board (commonly found on modems and printers).

DNS — Domain Name System is a database system for translating computer domain names into numeric Internet addresses.

Reference Section

Domain — Part of the naming hierarchy of the Internet.

Domain Name Server — Domain Name Servers enable domain names to be resolved into numerical IP addresses.

Down — Not working, as in "the BBS is down".

Download — The transfer of a file from another, remote, computer to your computer.

DTE — Data Terminal Equipment.

DTR — Data Terminal Ready, an RS-232C signal that is part of the handshake in a data transmission interface.

Duplex — A communications channel capable of carrying a signal in both directions.

EARN — European Academic Research Network.

EFF — Electronic Frontier Foundation, an American organisation that addresses the social and legal issues arising from the increased use of computer communications.

EMACS	One of the most common editors found on online systems.
Email	Electronic Mail. A method of sending messages via computer instead of the usual land based postal system. One of the most popular and important uses of computer communications.
Emote Icons	See "Smiley".
Encryption	A method of coding data to prevent unathorised access, most commonly used on the Internet to protect Email from prying eyes.
Equalisation	A compensation circuit built into some modems to offset distortion caused by the telephone channel.
Error Control	A variety of different techniques which check the reliability of characters or blocks of data.
Ethernet	A type of high speed local area network.
EUNet	European UNIX Network.
FAQ	A Frequently Asked Question. You will find FAQ files all over the Internet, in Usenet Newsgroups, mailing lists, at FTP, Gopher, and

Reference Section 133

File Server   A computer that stores files on the Internet, making them available for access by various Internet tools.

Finger   A program that displays the user, or users, on a remote system.

Firewall   A firewall is a security device to help protect a private network from Internet crackers and hackers. It is a machine with two network interfaces that is configured to restrict what protocols can be used across the boundaries and to decide what internal IP addresses can be seen to the external Internet.

Flame   An abusive or personal attack against the poster of a message. A flame is the online equivalent of losing your rag or thumping your teapot.

Flow Control   A technique to compensate for the differences in the flow of data input and output from a modem.

Fortune Cookie   See "Cookie".

#4 Teleworking .net

Forum	A message area on CompuServe or Delphi, equivalent to an echo on Fidonet, a newsgroup on USENET, or a conference on Cix.
Fragmentation	The process by which an IP datagram is broken into smaller pieces, so as to meet the requirements of a specific physical network.
Frame	A block of data with header and trailer information attached.
FreeNet	A popular method of providing "free" access to the Internet from the United States. Probably the most famous being the Cleveland FreeNet, which was also the first.
FTP	The File Transfer Protocol that defines how files are transferred over the Internet.
Full Duplex	Flow of information in both directions at the same time.
Gateway	A computer system to transfer data between otherwise incompatible networks.
Gibson, William	Author of "Neuromancer". Responsible for coining the term "Cyberspace".

Reference Section

Gopher	A menu based system for exploring the Internet.
Hacker	Someone who enjoys exploring computer systems, often applied to people who undertake such explorations illegally.
Half Duplex	Flow of information in both directions, but one way at a time.
Handshaking	An exchange of signals allowing communication between two devices, designed to start or keep the two in synchronisation.
Hayes	A modem manufacturer responsible for the first direct connection modems, and whose command set has become the industry standard.
Header	Part of a packet which precedes the actual data and contains source, destination, and error checking information.
Host	A computer that allows users to communicate with other computers on a network.
Hostname	The name given to a host computer.

HST	High Speed Technology. A proprietary signalling scheme used as part of the trademark for Miracom HST modems.
HTML	HyperText Mark-up Language, the language used to write a World Wide Web document.
HTTP	HyperText Transfer Protocol, used extensively by World Wide Web. Another of the many Internet protocols.
Hub	A device connected to many other devices.
Hz	Hertz. A measurement of frequency, each unit being one cycle per second.
IAB	The Internet Architecture Board, the "head honchos" if you like, who make decisions about Internet standards.
ICMP	Internet Control Message Protocol is the group of messages exchanged by IP modules in order to report errors.
Internet	Worldwide network of computer networks, connected using the IP protocol.

Reference Section

Internet Society — An organisation that exists to support the Internet, and also the governing body of the Internet Architecture Board.

IP — Internet Protocol on which the Internet is based.

IRC — Internet Relay Chat allows many users to chat in real time across the Internet.

ISDN — Integrated Services Digital Network combines voice and digital network services in one medium.

ISN — Initial Sequence Number is the first sequence number used on a TCP connection.

ITU-T — International Telecommunications UnionTelecommunications. The Telecommunications standards making organisation, which replaces the CCITT.

JANET — The Joint Academic NETwork of educational establishments in the UK.

JUNET — Japanese UNIX Network.

KA9Q	An implementation of TCP/IP for amateur packet radio systems.
Kermit	A file transfer protocol named after Kermit the Frog!
Kernel	The system commands containing level of an operating system or network system.
Kill File	A file which filters out any messages posted by those people named in it. If someone is in your kill file, you never see any messages from them again, hence you have effectively killed them. Seen in great numbers on USENET but also implemented in a growing number of Off Line Readers for various online systems.
Kit	Computer equipment.
Knowbot	The Knowbot Information Service is another method of trying to find where someone dwells within the Internet.
LAN	Local Area Network. A data network that serves a small area only.
Leased Line	A permanent connection between two sites, which requires no voltage on the line and no dialling.

Reference Section 139

LED	Light Emitting Diode. A device that emits light when electrical voltage is applied to it. Used on modem front panels as status indicators.
Line Noise	Disruption of computer communications caused by interference on the telephone line.
Lion Nose	See "Line Noise".
LISTSERV	An automated mailing list distribution system.
Local Echo	All transmitted data is sent to the screen of the sending computer.
Log	A record of file operations. In comms use, the storing to disk or file of an on-line session.
Login	The process of identifying yourself on an online system. Generally a two stage process involving the input of your username followed by your password.
Login Name	The "username" or name of your account used for identification purposes.
Lurker	Someone who reads but doesn't post in newsgroups, conferences,

or message areas. A sort of online voyeur.

Macro A macro instruction is a string or instruction replaced by a shorter string or instruction. In use this means you can execute a long sequence by typing just a short one.

Mail Gateway A machine that transfers mail between two or more email systems.

Mailing List A discussion group whose messages are distributed by email.

MHS Message Handling System.

MILNET The US MILitary NETwork.

MIME Mulitpurpose Internet Mail Extensions, a method of linking binary code into email.

MNP Microcom Network Protocol is a common modem error correction system.

Mode A specific condition or state under which a device may operate.

Modem MOdulator/DEModulator. A device to convert binary

Reference Section 141

	information into an analogue signal that can be transmitted over normal voice carrying telephone lines, and convert that signal back into computer readable data at the other end.
Moderator	The person who runs, or moderates, a conference or message area.
Mosaic	Probably the most commonly used World Wide Web graphical browser. Has been developed for many platforms, including Windows, Amiga, X-Windows, and Macintosh.
MTU	Maximum Transmission Unit is the largest unit of data that can be sent on a given system.
MUD	Multi User Dungeon, an online role playing adventure game.
MUG	Multi User Game, any online game where there are two or more players at the same time.
Net	Generally used as another name for the Internet, although sometimes people refer to both USENET and Cyberspace in general as "The Net".

#4 Teleworking .net

Netfind	A service that helps find email addresses for people on the Internet.
Net God	Someone who has achieved a "Godlike" status on the Net, either through the development of part of the Net or tools used in it, or because of their presence on the Net.
Net Police	A derogatory term applied to those people who feel it is their duty to tell others how they should behave in Cyberspace.
Net Surfer	Someone who "surfs" the Internet, wandering around looking for interesting places to visit, interesting files to grab, and interesting people to talk to.
Netiquette	The supposed etiquette of the online community, examples being avoiding overuse of quoting, avoiding cross posting, and so on.
Network	A group of computers that can communicate with each other.
Newbie	Someone who is a newcomer to a USENET group, often used as a term of ridicule or abuse.

Reference Section 143

Newsgroup	A message area, defined by subject matter, which forms part of USENET.
NFS	The Network File System. This allows use of files on remote network machines as if they were on your local machine.
NIC	Network Information Centre.
Node	A computer attached to a network.
NRAM	Non-volatile memory used by such devices as modems to store a user definable configuration which is read and acted upon at power up.
NSFNET	The National Science Foundation Network is one of the networks that makes up the Internet.
Null Modem	A cable used to directly connect two computers by their serial ports in which the transmitting and receiving pins are swapped.
Numeric Database	A database containing, specifically and unsurprisingly, numbers.
Offline	Not connected to an online system.

Off Line Reader	See "OLR".
OLR	Off Line Reader. A program that enables you to connect to an online system, download all your messages and email, read and reply to the offline and then send back your replies. An OLR can save you lots of money in telephone bills and online service charges, as well as provide in some cases a better user interface to the online system.
On-line	Refers to when two computers are connected by means of modems. For example, a Bulletin Board System is also an Online System.
Originate Mode	When the modem transmits in frequencies which are the reverse of the modem being called which is in answer mode.
Packet	A bundle of data.
Parity Bit	A check bit added to a unit of data for error checking purposes.
Password	A security string that is required to be input before access to a system, or part of a system, may be granted.

Reference Section 145

Phreaking — Making phone calls whilst bypassing the charging system. Phone phreaking was the forerunner to hacking as we understand it today.

PING — Packet Internet Groper is a program used to test destinations on the Internet to see if they exist, are operating, etc.

Plonk — The sound a newbie makes as he plummets to the bottom of a killfile list in a USENET group.

Pointer — A file marker so that an online system can remember what messages you have read when you disconnect, so you don't have to read them all again next time.

Polling — Connecting to another system to check for email and messages etc,

Port Number — Computers which run the TCP/IP protocols can use different ports to run different services. Each of these ports is allocated a specific number. Local services tend to be assigned on higher port numbers.

Post — To send a message, either by email or to a conference, message area, or newsgroup.

#4 Teleworking .net

Postmaster	The person responsible for taking care of mail across the Internet.
PPP	Point to Point Protocol. This allows a computer to use TCP/IP with a standard telephone line.
Profile	A control file for a program. Most commonly used to set up a user's individual preferences when logging onto an online service.
Protocol	Standards governing the transfer of information between computers. Developed to improve the reliability and speed of data transfer.
Public Domain	Software which is available to anyone without the requirement to pay for it.
Remote Echo	Everything the remote computer transmits is duplicated on your computer's screen.
REN	Ring Equivalent Number refers to a total figure which must not be surpassed by equipment connected to a single telephone socket.
REN and STIMPY	Happy Happy, Joy Joy.

Reference Section 147

Resume A text file containing personal information about a user of an online system, usually written by the user themselves.

RFC Request For Comments are sets of papers used for discussion on Internet standards.

ROT-13 A simple form of encryption, commonly applied to some USENET messages, which rotates the alphabet 13 places forwards or backwards.

Router A system that transfers information between two networks using the same protocols.

Scratchpad A temporary file used to hold messages whilst awaiting transfer or editing. Used on some online systems such as Cix.

Serial Cable The cable used to connect devices through a computer's serial port.

Serial Port The port that transmits and receives asynchronous data. Peripheral devices such as modems, printers, and mice can all use the serial port.

Server	A computer, or the software on that computer, that allows other computers to use it by means of client software.
Service Provider	Any organisation offering connections to the Internet, or part of it.
Shareware	Software which is generally available as "try before you buy" with the available version needing to be registered before its full power can be unleashed.
SIG	Special Interest Group, a forum or collection of forums on a particular subject. Found on on-line systems such as Delphi and CompuServe.
Signal to noise ratio	Used to describe the amount of on-topic postings as compared to the amount of wibble within a message area or conference.
Signature	A personal tag line used on the end of messages posted to online services. These can vary from a couple of words to many lines in length. Also known commonly as "sigs".

Reference Section

Site — Any of the individual networks that, as a whole, comprise the Internet.

SLIP — Serial Line IP is a protocol that allows a computer to use the Internet protocols using a standard telephone line.

Smiley — A smiling face character made by joining ASCII characters together. Used to express emotions etc. See the "Smiley Dictionary" in this book for more details.

SMTP — Simple Mail Transfer Protocol is used to transfer email between computers, as part of the TCP/IP protocol family.

Snail Mail — The sending of mail using the traditional land based postal system as opposed to email. So called because of its slowness compared to electronic mail.

Start/Stop Bits — Bits attached to a character before transmission during an asynchronous transfer.

Sterling, Bruce — Author mainly responsible for the coining of the term "Cyberpunk".

SysOp	SYStem OPerator, the person who runs a Bulletin Board System.
TCP	Transmission Control Protocol. One of the protocols upon which the Internet is based.
Teapot	One of my favourite words.
Teledildonics	The sexual act performed with the aid of Virtual Reality, computers, telecommunications and a couple of very sad and lonely people indeed.
Telnet	An Internet protocol that allows you to log in to other computer systems on the Net.
Thread	A series of postings to a message area or conference that are linked together. A thread consists of an initial posting followed by all the comments to it, and forms an online conversation or debate.
Throughput	The amount of data transmitted per second without the overhead of protocol information.
TLA	A Three Letter Acronym, although these are often found to contain more than three letters. Used to minimise typing and speed up

	communications. See the "TLA Dictionary" in this book for more details.
Topic	A subdivision of a conference, where the subject matter has been more distinctly defined. See entry for "Conference" for more details.
UDP	User Datagram Protocol, another of the protocols upon which the Internet is based.
UNIX	An operating system commonly used across the Internet.
Upload	The sending of a file from your computer to another, remote, computer.
URL	Uniform Resource Locator, an attempt to standardise the location or address details of Internet resources. Most commonly used, at the moment, in connection with the World Wide Web.
USENET	A group of systems that exchange debate, chat, etc in the form of newsgroups across the Internet.

UUCP	Unix to Unix copy is used for copying files between Unix systems.
UUencode	A method of encoding binary data so that it can be sent as an ASCII file across networks by Email. A decoder is required to convert the file back into an executable binary file again.
V.21	An ITU-T standard, a modem speed of 300bps.
V.22	An ITU-T standard, a modem speed of 1200bps.
V.22bis	An ITU-T standard, a modem speed of 2400bps.
V.23	An ITU-T standard, sending data at 75bps and receiving data at 1200bps.
V.32	An ITU-T standard, a modem speed of 9600bps.
V.32bis	An ITU-T standard, a modem speed of 14400bps.
V.34	An ITU-T standard a modem speed of 28800bps.
V.42	An ITU-T error correction standard.

Reference Section

V.42bis — An ITU-T error correction standard with data compression.

Veronica — An Internet tool that provides a Gopher menu that matched your keyword Gopher search.

Video Display — A monitor to those not talking techno-babbleTerminal.

Virtual Circuit — A logical transmission path.

Virtual Communities — A term that describes the communities that are very real, but exist only in computer networks. Another name for Cyberspace.

Virtual Reality — A computer technology that creates a very real illusion of being in an artificial world. Virtual Reality has already found its way into many real-life applications, from chemistry to architecture to games.

Virus — A program designed to infect and sometimes destroy other programs and computer equipment. Virus programmers are known, politely, as SMEEEEEEEEEEEEEGHEADS.

#4 Teleworking

WAIS	Wide Area Information Servers search databases across the INet.
WAN	A Wide Area Network as opposed to a Local Area Network.
White Pages	A list of Internet users, accessible through the Internet itself.
Whois	An Internet program to find out the email address etc of someone from a given name.
Wibble	Nonsense posted to a message area, conference, or newsgroup. Made into an art form by the likes of talk.bizarre on USENET and the norman conference on Cix.
World Wide Web	A hypertext based information and resource system for the Internet.
WWW	See "World Wide Web".
X.25	A packet switched data network, which is usually half-duplex.
X.29	Command set used to configure and establish X.25 connections.
X.400	ITU-T standard for email formats.
Zip	To archive a file or group of files using the PKZip archiver.

Index

Index

Acronyms	32, 119
Addresses (email)	41
Addresses (Internet)	37
Advertising	43
Advertising On-Line	102
Ameol	68
Anonymous FTP	47
Archie	49, 102
Auto-answer	28
BABT approval	12
Bandwidth	11
Baud rate	10, 20
Binary	8
BPS	10
BT Phonebase	107
Building regulations	76
Bulletin board	64
Business on the Internet (1)	102
Business on the Internet (2)	102
Business on the Internet (3)	102
Capital allowances	81
CityScape	59
Cix	19, 68, 107
CommUnity	110
Compression	11
CompuServe	69, 108
Computers	87
Conferences	67
Contents insurance	78
CPS	10
Data bits	21

.net Guide

Index

Databases 103
Delphi Internet 71, 108
Demon Internet 60
Demon Internet FTP..103
Direct Connection (The) 61
Domain 37
DTE 20

ELSPA...110
Email 40, 45
Entrepreneurs 103
Error correction..10

FAQ 32, 52
FAQ 52
FAST 110
Faxing 3, 12, 18
Fidonet 65
Files (sending & receiving)....................................26, 44
Flow control 21
FTP 39, 46
FTP by Email 103

Gopher 56

Hard disks...88
Hayes/AT commands 23
Home Run 98
Host mode...18, 28
HTML 53

Income Tax..80
Indemnity insurance 79
Internet 32

Internet Business Centre 104
Internet Business Journal 104
Internet connection (direct) 57
Internet connection (terminal-based) 57
Internet gateway 58
ISDN lines 90
ITU-T 9

Jargon 124

Leases 77
Loans 76

Macro 18
Macs 88
Mail-bombing 36
Mailing Lists (1) 104
Mailing Lists (2) 104
Mailing lists 50
Mailshots 43
Marketing 105
MIME 46
Modem speeds 113
Modems 8, 19
    External 13
    Installing a modem 15
    Internal 13
    Modem standards 9
    V standards 9
Moderator 52
Monitors 88
Mortgages 76

National Association of Teleworkers 98

Index

National Insurance Contributions 81
Net 32
Netscape 53
Node 37

OLR 67
On-line services 66
Optical character recognition 19
OwnBase 99

Parity 21
PC compatibles 87
Pension plans 80
Phone book 18
Planning permission 75
Planning regulations 74
POP 59
Postmaster 42
Protocols 17, 26

Review buffer 17
RS-232 87

Script 18
Searching 49, 55
Serial cable 14
Serial port 20, 87
Shareware 35, 48
Site name 37
Smartcom 18
Smileys 116
Software 17
Stop bits 21
SysOp 64

#4 Teleworking .net

Tax returns 82
TCP/IP 57
Telecottage Association 100
Telephone lines 89
Teleworking (1) 105
Teleworking (2) 105
Teleworking (3) 105
Teleworking 2, 74
Teleworking Special Interest Group 100, 106
Telnet 54
Thread 66

UNIX commands 114
Uploading 26
URL 101
Usenet 51
UUencoding 45

V standards 9
VAT 81
Veronica 56

WAIS 56, 106
WinCIM 67
Windows 87
World Wide Web 36, 53
World Wide Web Search Engine 106

Xmodem 27

Ymodem 17, 27

Zmodem 17, 27

Other Internet books from Future Publishing

This books forms part of a series of 12 Internet guides published by Future Publishing. We also publish an umbrella Internet title called 'All you need to know about the Internet', which costs £14.95 and comes with a free disk containing Chameleon Sampler, a demo suite of Internet software for PC owners.

'All you need to know about the Internet' is the perfect reference guide for newcomers to the Internet. It introduces all the activities you can engage in on the Net, including email, newsgroups, mailing lists, file transfer and much, much more.

All of these books are published in conjunction with Future Publishing's brand new UK-based .net magazine, which contains features for both experienced net users and newcomers. It features very high production and editorial quality, and is an essential source of information for those discovering the Internet's amazing potential. Retailing for £2.95, it's available at all good newsagents.

Future Publishing is committed to providing the best possible coverage of the Internet, which we believe is the computing revolution of the decade. Part of this coverage is this series of .net Guides, each targeted at specific Net users and needs. Each .net Guide consists of between 150-200 pages, is sized at 220mm (H) x 150mm (W) and retails at £7.95. Here is a list of all 12 titles:

.net Guide #1
All you need to know about Getting On-Line
by Toby Simpson
How to get on the Net quickly, easily and cheaply. No nonsense, no jargon, no hassle.
ISBN 1-898275-31-9
Publication Date December 1994

.net Guide #2
All you need to know about Communicating On-Line
by Davey Winder
Do you know 3 million people? You do now. Find out how to talk to people all over the world.
ISBN 1-898275-32-7
Publication Date November 1994

.net Guide #3
All you need to know about Using the Net
by Davey Winder
The Net software is your gateway to a world of information. Find out how to really use it.
ISBN 1-898275-33-5
Publication Date November 1994

.net Guide #4
All you need to know about Teleworking
by Simon Cooke
No commuting, no rush-hour... no boss? Find out how to work from home via the Net.
ISBN 1-898275-34-3
Publication Date April 1995

.net Guide

Other Internet books

.net Guide #5
All you need to know about On-Line Information
by Eddie Robinson
Forget your local library. The Net is the biggest source of information the world has ever seen. Find out how to get it.
ISBN 1-898275-35-1
Publication Date April 1995

.net Guide #6
All you need to know about Mailing Lists
by Davey Winder
Don't go searching for information – make it come to you. Keep up to date on anything from poodles to particle accelerators.
ISBN 1-898275-36-X
Publication Date January 1995

.net Guide #7
All you need to know about Setting up a BBS
by Toby Simpson
Find out how to run your own on-line service. What it costs, what to avoid – and how to make it a success.
ISBN 1-898275-37-8
Publication Date January 1995

net Guide #8
All you need to know about On-Line Gaming
by Davey Winder
Games consoles are history. Discover real gaming with real people in real situations. On-line gaming is the future.
ISBN 1-898275-38-6
Publication Date January 1995

#4 Teleworking .net

.net Guide #9
All you need to know about UK Internet Service Providers
by Davey Winder
You need a Service Provider. Find out who offers what and for how much.
ISBN 1-898275-39-4
Publication Date January 1995

.net Guide #10
All you need to know about The World Wide Web
by Davey Winder
Compare colour TV with long-wave radio. That's the WorldWide Web compared to the standard Net interface. Believe it.
ISBN 1-898275-40-8
Publication Date December 1994

.net Guide #11
All you need to know about Business On-Line
by Davey Winder
Good business is all about communication, expertise and commercial awareness. Find out how the Net will give you the edge.
ISBN 1-898275-42-4
Publication Date February 1995

.net Guide #12
All you need to know about Internet jargon
by Davey Winder
Baffled by jargon? Hacked off with technical terms? Every Internet buzz-word is explained right here. In plain English.
ISBN 1-898275-43-2
Publication Date February 1995

.net .net Guide

.net magazine subscription offer

Money back guarantee!

Save £5.50 and receive three trial issues! The normal subscription rate for .net magazine is £35.40, but readers of this book can subscribe at the special rate of £29.90!

If you are not fully satisfied after you've received these three trial issues you are entitled to a full money-back refund.

.net is your monthly guide to the Internet, helping you to make sense of the jargon and guiding you to the best that the Net has to offer. Whether you're looking for something new or weird, for leisure or business, .net magazine will take you there.

Regular "How-to" guides combine with in-depth features every month to give you the chance to thoroughly explore the Net without the trouble or trauma normally associated with going on-line.

Take out a no-risk subscription to .net magazine NOW.

Subscribe now and you'll **SAVE** over **£5 OFF** the price that you'd normally pay at the newsagents and get every issue delivered direct to your home. We're sure that you'll love .net so we're happy to give you a no-risk guarantee: If you are in any way unhappy with .net then you can cancel your subscription at any time and receive a full refund. Complete and return the subscription form right away or

telephone: 01225 822511 or
e-mail: subs@futurenet.co.uk

(See overleaf for subscription order form)

#4 Teleworking the internet magazine **.net**

Subscription order form

the internet magazine .net

Yes, please accept my subscription to .net magazine at a **saving** of **£5.50**. I understand that I may cancel my subscription if not fully satisfied after receiving my first three issues for a full money-back refund*.

(*This offer is available to UK residents only. Overseas rates are available on application. Please note the deadline for cancellation is one week after receipt of your third issue.)

Title (Mr/Mrs/Miss) _____ Initials _____ Surname _____

Address _____

_____ Postcode _____

Method of payment (please tick one):

☐ Access   ☐ Visa   ☐ Cheque   ☐ Postal order

Credit card no _____

Expiry date _____

Signature _____ Date _____

☐ Tick here if you do not wish to receive details of future **.net** products.

Send this form to **.net Subscriptions, Future Publishing Ltd, FREEPOST (BS4900), Somerton, Somerset TA11 6BR**

the internet magazine .net .net Guide